Happy Days

Happy Days

NATALIE CASSIDY

ONE PLACE. MANY STORIES

HQ
An imprint of HarperCollins*Publishers* Ltd
1 London Bridge Street
London SE1 9GF

www.harpercollins.co.uk

HarperCollins*Publishers*
Macken House, 39/40 Mayor Street Upper,
Dublin 1, D01 C9W8, Ireland

This edition 2025
1
First published in Great Britain by HQ,
an imprint of HarperCollins*Publishers* Ltd 2025

Printed and bound in the UK using 100% Renewable Electricity by CPI Group (UK) Ltd

For more information visit: www.harpercollins.co.uk/green

For my daughters, Eliza and Joanie.
Everything I do is for you.

Foreword

First of all, I'd like to thank you for picking up my book. Wow, it's hard to believe those words when I read them back, to be honest. I've written a book. Little old me! I'm someone who feels ridiculously pleased with myself for going on a run, or making chutney for the first time, so you can imagine how great this feels, especially as it's something I've always wanted to do.

I'm fascinated by time, dates and numbers, so what you're about to read is set out as a book of days, a kind of personal almanac based around the days of the week and special occasions like Christmas, which is my absolute favourite time of the year. It's a trip through the highs and lows of daily life and the changing seasons, but it's also my thoughts on some of the lessons I've learned over the years in my different phases: grief, diets, body image, mum-guilt, smartphones, fame, smudged mascara, cooking, and bringing up strong-minded girls are some of the subjects I tackle head on. Since I love nothing more than a good story, there's loads of those as well, plus tips, hints, lists and anything else I think would fit the mix to make up a tasty charcuterie board of topics.

You can't eat it unfortunately, but it's the sort of book you can dip into or read straight through – and hopefully, it'll last longer that way. I'm also hoping it will get you thinking about how to take pleasure in the day-to-day rhythm of life and find different ways to be content. Life is wonderful, even when you've got all that other stuff going on, so, let's make the most of it.

Happy days.

Thank you for reading!

The Twelfth of Never

'There are seven days in a week and *someday* isn't one of them.'

When you're ten years old, forty feels like an unreachable age. It's fine for other people to be forty, of course – adults, parents, teachers, whoever . . . But your own fortieth birthday seems so far off that the chance of you ever getting there is as likely as a week of back-to-back sunshine in February.

And then, before you know it, there it is. The unimaginable landmark – at least, to your ten-year-old self. You're about to turn forty! And where does this milestone find you?

As my fortieth loomed in May 2023, I was in a good place. Although my parents had both passed away and I was still grieving the loss of my dad, my home life was really happy and I had a great job that gave me financial security.

Yet, in the months leading up to my birthday, I could feel myself getting restless for change. I'd been playing Sonia Fowler in *EastEnders* on and off for nearly thirty years, since I was ten, and I'd loved every moment of it. But thirty years is a long time to play such a defining role, and now, approaching this big milestone, I realised that what I really wanted was to spend more time being me, Natalie. To branch out and explore new things.

In fact – and I only half realised it in the moment – the change was already happening. I had dipped my toe into different projects over the years, doing plays, sitcom cameos, quiz shows and reality TV. Now, I was being invited onto various people's podcasts as a guest, going here and there to talk about this and that.

One day I stopped and thought, 'I really enjoy this.'

It was my niece Maria who planted the seed: 'You're really good at podcasts, Nat. I don't know why you don't have your own.'

Her comment got me thinking, but I also knew how hard it could be to steer your life in a new direction. When you're a mum, you tend to put family first; you don't want to shake things up too much.

I gave myself some time to think about it. I'm quite good at mulling things over, especially when it comes to making important decisions. Your foundations are generally laid at forty, aren't they? You've developed a solid sense of who you are; you know who your friends are and what's important in life. It's not the case for everyone, of course, but even if you haven't got things completely sorted or settled, you have enough experience to know what's what. And hopefully you're a little bit wiser and more confident than you used to be . . .

Still, the idea of starting my own podcast was daunting. It felt like a big risk. Even though I was prepared to put a lot of planning into it, I had no idea know how it would turn out and was very conscious that it could end in failure – and being in the public eye means that your failures are out there for all to see. But I felt I had to give it a go. You don't want to get to seventy and think, 'I never tried that.'

It was scary, and hard to undertake, but I made the leap. I converted our spare bedroom into a recording studio for my podcast. I bought a table and some recording equipment; I got someone in to cover the windows with muslin and muffle the walls with more muslin. Now, I have a space in my house reserved for me, my own world, where I keep in touch with my podcast community and put the world to rights, and share this newfound passion with my family members, who are fully on board and a huge part of it. And I'm loving it.

It's been incredible doing the podcast and seeing a community of people grow around it. It has opened up other possibilities, as well – like writing this book, something my ten-year-old self would have been amazed at. Honestly, I'm pinching myself, even now; I'm so grateful for all the opportunities that have come my way.

Looking back, I think I've always been quite brave; I've done things that some people wouldn't do, including leaving a horrible relationship when I was younger. That's something that can be really difficult, which is why so many people stay put even when they know deep down it would be better to leave. It takes courage to walk away.

I've also had to brush off a lot of negative comments about my looks and clothes, online and in the press, which is of course inevitable when you grow up on the telly, like I did. I think I've been quite brave in that way, too. At this point, I'm pretty sure I've got elephant skin, after all the things that people have come out with about me and my looks. My favourite saying is, 'What people think of you is none of your business.'

But this new courage to say, 'Right, come on, you can do whatever you want to do. Just do it!' has only come later on in life, as I've become that much more sure of who I am and what I want.

It's also about realising how precious time is and how short life can be – something you think about more as you start getting older. I've always been really aware of it, having lost my mum at a young age. There comes a moment when you say to yourself, 'Well, what are you waiting for? There's no time like the present.'

Don't leave it until the Twelfth of Never . . .

Chapter One

Monday

I'm a curious person, so I'm going to start this book with a question: is one day any different from another? Isn't every day the same?

OK, that's two questions – and you might ask why I'm writing a book of days if I can't answer either of them. But, really, how do you distinguish a Monday from a Wednesday? It's just hours, minutes and seconds; it's just time.

Monday for me is simply another day of being lucky to be alive. The same goes for Tuesday or Sunday. It's a day for thinking, 'Oh, I'm here again. That's good. Thank you.'

Even if you've woken up on the wrong side of the bed, you can't argue with the idea that human existence is miraculous. Did you know that your chances of being born are one in 400 trillion? Amazing. One hundred and fifty generations of couples had to meet and get pregnant in order to produce you, and a particular egg had to join with a particular sperm roughly every twenty-five years since the Stone Age to bring forth your unique cluster of genes and DNA.

Even before that, humans had to evolve over aeons and

aeons from a one-cell blob into this unbelievably complex machine that just keeps going and going – the human body. How did that happen? I don't think anybody really knows how the brain keeps our blood pumping and our organs quietly functioning while fretting about work, childcare, maybe buying a new jacket and what to cook for tonight's dinner. And if you want to drive a car and wiggle your toes at the same time, the brain can do that, too. It's mind-blowing!

Everything about our existence is incredible. We're spinning through space on a giant piece of rock with billions of stars and planets all around us, a speck on a speck in the middle of an unimaginably vast solar expanse that we know next to nothing about. Our planet just happens to have the perfect combination of gases in its atmosphere to give us air to breathe, water to keep us hydrated, plants growing, animals roaming and awe-inspiring sunsets. Plus, we've invented banana holders to stop our fruit getting bruised. We've *really* lucked out. So why are we worried about what day it is?

Is it because we like to label things? Days have had names for as long as people have written things down. The Ancient Egyptian week was divided into ten days, the Etruscan week was eight days and then in 321 CE, the Roman Emperor Constantine introduced the seven-day week. The Romans named their days after the Sun, the Moon and five planets in our galaxy that were also gods: Mars, Mercury, Jupiter, Venus and Saturn.

The English weekday names are a mishmash handed down from our Roman and Viking invaders. The Latin, *dies solis,* means 'day of the sun' and eventually became *sunnudagr* in Anglo Saxon, named after Sunna the Norse sun goddess. And *dies lunae* means 'moon day', which became *manadagr,* after Mani, the man in the moon. The rest of the days (except Saturday) are named after the Norse gods, Tyw, Wodin, Thor and Frigg.

A lot of songs have been written about Monday, but do any of them capture its essence, if it has one? Because they all seem to express different moods and feelings. Depending on who's singing about it, a Monday can be stormy, manic, depressing or full of joy.

And that seems about right really, because anything can happen on a Monday. The best and the worst can happen: my lovely mum passed away on a Monday, and I also had my first date with my other half, Marc, on a Monday. Talk about extremes.

And yet Monday, being the start of the week, makes us think of new beginnings and of turning over a new leaf. It's almost like a mini New Year's Day, and we get one every week – although I have to wonder why we think of it like that. Surely you can make a fresh start any time?

'It's Monday,' we think. 'This week's going to be different from last week.' *Is it, though?*

Saying that, I do love a Monday when I open my diary and it's a new week and a clean page. I love having a physical, paper diary – I don't go anywhere without it. Turning over from the week before feels like having a fresh exercise book at school at the beginning of term. The smell of new paper, the spotless blank pages. Thinking to yourself, 'Wow, I must keep it neat.' For me, that good intention lasts for about two hours, then before you know it, there are doodles everywhere! Endless hearts and flowers. I find a lot of fresh starts end that way, with good intentions that I haven't quite seen through.

Why do people feel they can start things properly on a Monday, rather than simply doodling along? Why don't they say, 'We're going to start the diet on a Wednesday?' Although, quite frankly, don't bother starting a diet at all because none of them ever last, whatever day you decide on.

I don't know why I doodle endless hearts and flowers, but maybe there's a connection with the old Max Miller song, 'Hearts and Flowers', that I used to sing as a kid. Dad had one of his vinyl records, and I knew it back to front; I used to stand in the middle of the lounge and perform it all the way through. To be fair, I also sang Kylie and Jason songs, and Wham!, and tunes from *Oliver!* and *Me and My Girl*. But Max Miller was one of Dad's faves, along with Frank Sinatra and Nelson Riddle, and I shared his old-fashioned tastes.

Max Miller was a household name from the 1920s until his death in 1963. Known as 'The Cheeky Chappie', he was a genius stand-up comedian who topped the bill at the Hackney Empire and other great music hall venues. As part of his routine, he often wouldn't finish a joke but leave the punchline to your imagination. Then, with precise comic timing, he'd accuse you of having immoral thoughts. It was a clever way round the censors of the age.

Two Max Miller Jokes:
A husband came home one night, and his wife was there, and standing next to her was a fella without a stitch on.
'What on earth is going on?'
'He's a nudist, and he's come in to use the phone.'

And . . .
'Mary had a little bear
To which she was so kind.
I often see her bear in front . . .
'Ere, it's people like you who give me a bad name!'

Now that we're talking about beginnings, it seems a good moment to say that I had a great start in life. I felt loved and cared for in my early years, and really, that's all that matters to you when you're a kid. I have such a warm feeling whenever I think of my mum and a big part of me leans towards being more like her. I'm sure she's the reason I have an obsession with trying to have a nice home.

My mum was born Evelyn Elizabeth Bellamy and people called her 'Ev', except my dad, who called her 'Liza', which is where my Eliza gets her name from. Mum and Dad met around 1950, when she was twelve and he was fifteen. Her dad, my granddad Bellamy, who I never met, had a paper shop in St Peter's Street, Islington, and my dad, Charles William

Cassidy, worked in the shop when he was a young teen. Mum and Dad were childhood sweethearts. They got married in 1963 and loved each other their whole lives.

My mum was forty-four when she had me in 1983. My dad was forty-six and my two older brothers, Tony and David, were fifteen and eighteen.

Despite their ages, I'm told I was very much a planned baby. My mum said to my dad, 'The house is going to be empty when the boys go. I'd like another one.'

My parents were both absolutely thrilled when I came along. My brothers weren't so impressed, though. When my dad sat in the car with them and said, 'We're going to have another little mouth to feed,' they thought they were getting a puppy! My brothers were disgusted when they found out they were getting me instead, but once I arrived, they cherished me, and at times, it felt a bit like I had three dads growing up, because of the age gap.

When I think back to the early days of my childhood, I can draw a direct line between the little girl I was then and who I am now – someone who loves entertaining and making people laugh. We spent a lot of evenings in hospitals when I was seven and eight because both my nans were poorly around that time, but I didn't mind it; in fact, being a little performer even then, I was in my element, entertaining all the oldies on the ward, belting out their favourite songs and larking around.

Who did I think I was? Well, I certainly didn't get my performing gene from my mum or dad, who weren't like that at all, although people always describe my mum as having been 'a character'. Mum had a cheeky smile and was full of humour. She liked a wind-up and a laugh, and people remember her as a lovely lady, especially in the way she held herself and the way she spoke about her kids. I remember Mum chatting to the staff in M&S, and Tony on the veg stall in Chapel Market – she always had time for people, and I'm very much that way, too. I love to stop and chat!

I was Little Miss Curious as a kid, and my favourite film was the Disney production of *Alice in Wonderland*. Today I'm a bit of an autodidact, so no matter where I am, I'll always buy a book about the place. If I'm in Rome, I want to know about the history; if I go to Bath, I'm looking at property prices because I'd like to move there. When I see a painting, I want to know about the artist. I'm fascinated by history, especially art history, and all the distinctive people who have made an impact in their different ways down the ages.

Mum used to say I was an old soul. She said I was the sort of child who looks at you and you think, 'Oh, you've been here before!' I had a knowing look, a twinkle in my eye, and I was cheeky, like Mummy.

Being an old soul is also having a love of old-fashioned things, and for me, that comes from having older parents. It's the music you grow up with, the TV you watch, the comedy you find funny and your surroundings that make that difference. For instance, I like old-fashioned decor styles, all floral prints, chintz and rich velvets. The other morning, I put Ella Fitzgerald on and thought, 'I'd have a gramophone if I could.'

Of course, what I actually do is shout, 'Alexa, put on Ella Fitzgerald.' But at heart, I'm not a very modern person really.

My dad was more serious than my mum. Dad's last remaining brother, Uncle George, would laugh if I said that Daddy was a miserable sod, because he was, but in a lovable way. He was a clever man, very private, and I had a really special and close relationship with him. I was a real daddy's girl.

My granddad was a tic-tac man; an arm-waving bookie at the horses. He was one for being in the pubs, on the piano and a bit of a drinker, so maybe performing is in the blood, I don't know – I never got to meet him. One of my brothers, Tony, is a natural entertainer and the other, David, is a brilliant joke teller, so it could be inherited, I suppose. But I think it's just as possible that my obsession with comedy and stand-up started with Dad's Max Miller record, along with the hearts and flowers doodles all over my diary.

And talking of humour . . .

I grew up watching the comedy and sitcoms that my parents watched: *The Two Ronnies*, *Porridge*, *Open All Hours*, *Only Fools and Horses* and *Fawlty Towers*. There was *'Allo 'Allo!*, *Birds of a Feather*, *French and Saunders*. Marc was the same. It's amazing that I've met someone who's as obsessed with sitcoms as I am. Our kids love them, too: Joanie is obsessed with *Only Fools and Horses*. They love comedy because we love comedy, and for us it's *Friday Night Dinner*, which is great. Some people may not find *Friday Night Dinner* appropriate for a nine-year-old. However, I would rather her sat with me with certain crude jokes going over her head, than her sat over there with her eyes glued to a tablet.

I missed *Blackadder*, probably because my dad didn't like it and so it wasn't on at home. My brother loves Monty Python, but I didn't go that way, either. My mum and I loved *Absolutely Fabulous*. I had all the AbFab videos. There was *Friends*, as well, which gives me a safe, warm feeling of nostalgia when it comes on, although I don't watch it much now. I'm a big Laurel and Hardy fan, probably because it used to be on BBC Two all through the summer holidays.

OK, I'm still pondering whether or not Monday is the best day for a fresh start. It's the first day of the week, so it's got that in its favour – although not if you live in the US, Israel or South Asia, where the first weekday is Sunday. It's a puzzle: which is the real first day of the week? What if the Big Bang had happened on a Thursday? Would it have changed anything? And if God created light on the first day, was it a Sunday or a Monday?

The very first thing on my Monday list most weeks is getting the kids up and off to school. That's a start of a kind, if not a particularly fresh one. It's a start-again, the beginning of a new and yet oh-so familiar cycle of yelling, 'Bag packed? Got all your books? PE kit? Ukulele?'

I'm lucky in that my kids are very self-sufficient now. Gone are the days of refusing to put on their shoes at the last minute, or tantrums about the bobbly seam in the toe of one of their socks, and I'm quite glad about that. I nearly threw Eliza out of the window once, after forty-five minutes of pleading with her to 'Please put the sock on!' What a waste of time!

My Joanie is a great example of what we all want to feel like on a Monday. In fact, it doesn't matter what day it is – she jumps out of bed between five-thirty and six-thirty every morning without fail, and she's full of beans, full of ideas, full of exploration. She'll stand none-to-nose with me and talk about all the things she's got in her brain. My eyes are barely open, but I love her for her joy for life. Obviously, I'm biased because she's my nine-year-old. (I really can't believe she's nine already. Where does the time go?) I'm sure that lots of children her age are the same way, but I think we should all try to hold on to some of that sparkle and fizz, even as we grow older.

Like most teenagers, my eldest, Eliza, has had her moments when it comes to growing up. She's getting better, but I actually think you need to give teenagers a break because there's a lot going on for them. I think it's ridiculous the amount they are supposed to do educationally when their hormones are going through the roof. It should all come a bit later, I feel, when they're more settled and can have a clearer sense of what they want.

I love my time with Eliza and Joanie in the mornings, but don't get me wrong – our breakfast table isn't laid out perfectly like in a hotel, and I'm often begging Eliza to eat a banana in the car. It always feels good once I've got them into school and I can breathe out and know I've got some time to myself while they're safe somewhere else. When I see mums crying at the school gate on the first day of term as they wave their kids off, I can't help but think, 'Is that real?'

I'm not talking about the first ever day your child goes to school, when we all probably shed a tear or two, because it's such a big milestone in their lives and they suddenly seem to have gone from being a toddler to a proper child. No, I'm talking about full-on weeping and separation anxiety that some people seem to have on the first day of the spring term in Year Three. What's that all about?

It makes me feel guilty. 'Maybe I'm not normal,' I think.

Last year, I missed the girls' first day back at school after the summer holidays because I had to work. Marc was at home; he sent me lovely pictures of them by the door with their uniforms on, and I realised I didn't feel bad after all – I had to go to work, and you can't just not go to work because the kids are going back to school.

In our house, there's often some anxiety in the air around the start of the autumn term, but I don't know if that's about the emotion of the kids going back to school, or something else? I always think that you can sense the passing of time in September – the seasons are changing, the summer is over and the long, light days are coming to an end. There's nostalgia too: you remember your own school days, and there's a sense of the kids growing up and moving up to the next year.

I don't think we should feel upset when the kids begin their new school year, though. They've had six whole weeks at home! It's a long time for a child, and they're ready to go back. In my mind, I think four weeks would be a better length of time for the summer holidays, because they seem to forget how to do everything after six. I think it would be great if we could spread the holidays out a bit over the year – I'd love another week at Christmas! Two weeks never feels like enough time for Christmas, whereas six weeks in the summer is ages.

In terms of beginnings, though, I honestly feel like the start of the school year is more important than actual New Year. It's an exciting time. The kids are going to have six hours a day with their friends, and they're going be using their brains. It's a new stage for them, and ultimately, that's a good thing. You also get some time back from worrying about keeping them entertained all day or finding childcare. If you're feeling sad or anxious about it, try and turn it on its head. Look at it positively and think: 'I'm grateful for a lovely summer. I'm so excited for them. Let's hope they have a lovely year with nice friends, and that they learn loads.'

I like getting back to an empty house after school drop-off on a Monday morning, especially if I've done a quick clean the night before. I relish that take-a-breath moment of calm and quiet once the morning rush is over. Often, I will have gone to bed early the night before, after a lovely long day of cooking, eating, and having the family round for a Sunday roast. I've slept well and I'm feeling fresh and ready to conquer the world with only the minimum of make-up applied. Saying that, I could easily have a bit of a fuzzy head on a Monday morning, if it was a really big lunch with family and friends. But it's nothing a cup of tea can't sort out, and then it's time to open the diary, make some calls or go for a walk. Whenever I have a spare hour, I love nothing more than seeing one of my dear friends for a coffee or a wander and an hour of chat before getting on with our days. Not only are you getting your steps in, but you're also catching up, having a laugh, a moan, talking about your plans or what you're cooking for dinner. It's a little bit of therapy.

It's great being at home on a Monday morning. Of course, I might not be, and that's okay, too. It used to be that mums were at home and dads were off to work, but for lots of us, it's not like that these days. I could be anywhere. Like many people, my job doesn't often allow me to plan or have a routine, because every day is different. These days, I could be acting, recording my podcast or a voiceover, doing an interview, reading or researching . . . I can't even think of all the different things I might be booked to do, regardless of what day of the week it is. Very occasionally, when things get really frantic, a car will arrive to pick me up for something and I have to check with the driver where it is we're actually going! That doesn't happen often though, because I am obsessive about my diary and keeping on top of what's what – we have to be, as mums, when we're all juggling so much.

A lot of us have lives that keep us on our toes, don't we? With or without work commitments, we're all extremely busy, spinning plates. We're looking after our children; we're caring for elderly parents, or siblings; we have partners that we'd like to see at least once in a while; or we have friends in need and want to help them. We're worrying about money, we're worrying about everybody else and we may have our own medical things going on at the same time. It's a lot.

But that Monday thing is just ingrained. Whether you like it or not, we are programmed to start things on a Monday. I'm as guilty of it as anyone. One Monday morning not so long ago, I thought to myself, 'Starting today, I'm going to be good about what I eat this week.' How many Mondays have I said that?

It didn't work out because I hadn't looked at my diary and so I didn't realise that I was booked on a job I'd forgotten about. And the best bit of this job was sitting down to a delicious roast dinner! A juicy leg of duck, potatoes, veg and gravy, washed down with a glass of really good red wine, followed by pudding and cheese. Not bad for a day's work, but bang went my good intentions. I had to put off my new regime until the next day. It was a real turn up for the books.

'Ah,' you're asking, 'but did you?'

'Did I what?'

'Did you start again on the Tuesday?'

Well, no, I didn't. Because the week ran away with me, and I forgot about all about my plans to start the week off right. But I could have started again. It doesn't have to be a Monday to turn over a new leaf. Look, if you were going into hospital for a heart transplant and the surgeon told you that it would be a brand-new start for you after years of ill health, never in a million years would you say, 'Well, it'll have to wait until Monday.' That's all I'm saying: why can't you choose to go in a completely new direction mid-morning on a Tuesday?

If you don't start the off week well, though, I do find that it can be hard to pick things up the next day, and if you haven't done it by Wednesday – forget it. And sometimes life is too short – today or any day. You know what it's like. There are so many things to worry about, so let's not beat ourselves up about breaking our resolutions, guys. Not until next week, anyway!

Monday is named after a mythological personification of the moon. But is that person female or male? In Egyptian mythology, the moon and the sun are ruled by male deities: Khonsu and Ra. Where's the balance in that?

In Ancient Greece, the moon was called Selene, and also Cynthia. (Hello!) In Rome, it was another female, Luna. In Norse mythology, it's a man in the moon, Mani, and the moon is viewed as male in cultures ranging from Japan to Australia. But in wellness forums, I'd say the trend definitely leans towards a female moon. You can basically take your pick.

The moon has strong associations with fertility, tides, gravity, psychology, sleep, calendars, crime and werewolves. It's contradictory because you can 'moon' over someone romantically or send quite the opposite message by 'mooning' them . . .

Just giving you something to ponder on a Moonday, guys . . . !

Monday is the start of the working week, and I grew up with a dad who worked his socks off, first in a bank and then in the paper shop business. When I was little, it was a shop in St John Street in the City of London, which was thirty minutes from our house in Dagmar Terrace in Islington if you walked it, which Dad always did. It was a really tough job – he'd be up and out of the house at four o'clock in the morning, back home at seven o'clock at night, six days a week – but he did it without complaint so that he could provide for his family. We had nice things when I was growing up, and that was important to him, as well. Dad spoiled my mum, in the best possible way. He wanted her to have nice jewellery and anything else that would make her eyes light up.

Mum was a smart lady, very well turned out. She was always laden with gold jewellery and a few diamonds, but her look was understated rather than glam. Everything was from M&S. Her hair was neatly styled but she didn't wear a lot of make-up. When she went out, she'd either wear a long skirt with a blouse and a jacket, or trousers and a jacket. She was never in jeans or a tracksuit.

Mum was a stay-at-home mother, a housewife, and she found a lot of contentment in the domestic sphere. She loved her home and bringing up the children, dressing them nicely and cooking a roast dinner on a Sunday. That was her pride and joy – her home and her family – and she was brilliant at it.

I'm not saying it was easy for her. Being a housewife is a full-time job, and on top of looking after me and my brothers, Mum looked after and cared for her mum, who was poorly. Mum's mum, my Nanny Liz, lived with us for many, many years and Mum could never leave her by herself. She took great pride in caring for Nanny Liz. In my earliest memories, Nanny Liz is always in the room and Mum is always at home, except the times when we were all up at the hospital. If Nanny Liz was in her room, I'd take her up a Guinness and read to her from my joke book and make her laugh. We watched *Birds of a Feather* together, and whenever I hear that theme tune now, I'm transported back to Nanny's room.

I feel very lucky that I had such a loving, stable upbringing. My parents were the best mum and dad I could have asked for. I think I'm a fifty-fifty split between them: I'm quite a character, like my mum, but also serious and hardworking, like my dad.

My 'Living at Home' Top 5 Songs

- 'Ocean Drive' – Lighthouse Family
- 'How About You?' – Frank Sinatra
- 'I Won't Last a Day Without You' – The Carpenters
- 'The Winner Takes It All' – ABBA
- 'I've Got You Under My Skin' – Frank Sinatra

Music of my Childhood

- My mum and dad were into The Carpenters, ABBA and Frank Sinatra.
- My brother Tony loved Pink Floyd and New Order.
- My brother David loved soul music and The Jam and Madness. I loved it all.

I was practically an only child growing up because Tony moved out a few years after I was born and David went even earlier. So, I was surrounded by adults and older people throughout my childhood, which probably made me a bit of an old soul. I wasn't blessed with a sister, but something in the universe said, 'I'll tell you what we're going to give you instead: two sister-in-laws who are as good as sisters, because they've known you since you were a baby, and three amazing nieces on top.'

My sister-in-law Linda remembers the day my brother David told her I'd been born, and I've literally known her all my life. The two of us can talk for hours and hours and never get bored. She's amazing. Tony's wife, Sharon, is wonderful, and my nieces Maria, Ellia and Evie are just fantastic. Evie May is younger and will call me 'Auntie'. But Maria is David's first child and came along when I was three, so we're more like sisters, and Ellia and I also get on unbelievably well. It's hard to express my feelings for Maria and Ellia. They are my sisters; my best friends. I'm their auntie; they're my nieces. It's an amalgamation of everything you could want. If I go a day without talking to Ellia or Maria, I feel depressed. I don't know if it's a good thing or not to feel like that, but it's how I feel: I need that connection and I don't know what I'd do without them.

Songs That Remind Me of My Nieces

- 'Ain't No Mountain High Enough' – Marvin Gaye and Tammi Terrell

- 'Big Fun' – The Gap Band
- 'Foundations' – Kate Nash
- 'Stay' – Lisa Loeb
- 'You Can Call Me Al' – Paul Simon
- 'Turn Your Love Around' – George Benson
- 'Jambalaya' – The Carpenters

I wish I had stronger memories of my mum, but she passed away when I was nineteen, and memories fade over the years. I can only recall my childhood up to the age of twelve or thirteen in vivid detail because once you're a teenager, you're off and out and about and mainly interested in yourself, so I feel like I only had those early years with her.

Mum left me her gold jewellery, and I love wearing certain pieces. I think of her as I put them on and it's reassuring to be aware of them as I go about my day. It's like having a little piece of her with me. I felt a real sense of responsibility to keep her jewellery in the family and divide it up fairly between her grandchildren, so when Maria got married, I gave her a couple of her Nanny Ev's gold charms, and when Evie May turned twenty-one, I gave her a gold bracelet of Nanny's. It feels nice to do the things that maybe Mum would have done, even though she's not here to do it herself.

It's such a sadness for me that my mum passed before I'd had time to circle back to her in my twenties. My brothers say it was the same for them – they went off in their teens and weren't interested in our parents, but, being that much older than me, they came back to Mum before it was too late. I feel guilty because I lost her at an age when she wasn't the most important person in my life, and I would have loved to have been able to spend time with her in my twenties. We never got to go shopping and have lunch or push the pram round the park together when I became a mum myself. With each passing year, I feel the loss of her more deeply. It makes me realise how precious time – and life – is.

One thing I could never forget is standing in the kitchen with Mum while she was making pastry. It's such a lovely, warm memory – for me, it captures the essence of Mum and the way she provided everything I needed during my childhood. I'm so grateful to her for the love and care she gave me, and for her wonderful homemaking and cooking. I can't help feeling that the foundation I was given by my parents has kept me grounded through everything that has happened to me since.

Mum was a feeder. She'd put out piles of sandwiches and trays of tea for me and my friends when they came over to our house: mountains of ham sandwiches, tea and biscuits, chocolate rolls, jam tarts, you name it. She cooked a lot of things from scratch – lots of meat pies and suet puddings, and her apple pie and custard was the best I have ever tasted. My favourite was stuffed pig's hearts! I imagine that Mum's meat creations were learned from her grandmother, who had an offal stall in Chapel Market. My love of offal remains to this day. When I'm at my local pub, it's kidneys on toast for me. You can turn up your nose if you like, but I love it!

My mum never seemed to have a problem with deciding

what to cook, and it felt like there was a constant rotation of delicious meals served up at home, but now that I'm in charge of picking what's for tea, I just can't think of anything to make my kids! My mind goes blank, and I fall back on the first thing that I think of. Then they'll say, 'My God, are we having this *again*?'

Maria used to come and stay with us for weeks on end in the summer or at Christmas, and I loved it. Our favourite game was pretending to present a cooking show programme using Play-Doh as our ingredients. Preparing food seemed so easy in the days when you didn't actually eat what you'd made! I have so much respect for the hard work Mum put into her cooking now that I know how much time and effort it takes.

These days, me, Maria and Ellia will often text each other on our WhatsApp group: 'What are you having tonight? I need inspiration.'

I must have two-hundred odd cookery books, yet all I can ever seem to think of to make is cod and chips, chilli and rice, or chicken fajitas. The carousel goes round and round in our house.

Don't feel bad if you're feeling uninspired, though. It's all about time. We're not living in the 1950s where Dad's out at work and Mum's got all day to prepare a home-cooked meal, and then you all sit down together as a family. It's a rarity in this day and age to sit down for a meal together on a weekday. At least my children have always loved vegetables. They eat green beans, cauliflower, broccoli and carrots. I also want to get them onto the courgettes and aubergines, but maybe that's asking too much right now. It probably is, thinking about it. On holiday a couple of summers ago, we were in an all-inclusive hotel in Greece with a buffet to die for. It was beautiful: a honeycomb dripping with sweetness, balls of burrata, fruit salad, feta cheese, watermelon . . . just stunning. And every morning, Joanie would come back from the buffet with a plate piled with bacon, and a plain croissant. I couldn't believe it! I've never been so embarrassed.

On a weekday night, the idea of cooking can often make me feel overwhelmed, so I'll go to the freezer and get out a meal that Marc has batch-cooked. I love the idea of batch cooking, but I don't get around to it enough. Marc's quite good at it though, and when he does a curry or a chilli or a shepherd or cottage pie, he'll always make more than we can eat and freeze the rest. That's the secret, isn't it? Just do the dinner, but double it up, and then it doesn't feel like batch cooking. If I can get a bit more organised with my diary, I would love to spend a day in the kitchen every now and then and make a few meals for Marc and the kids to eat when I'm at work. It makes things easy for everyone and saves money, too.

I had two lovely free hours at home the other day and so I made a lasagna. I cooked my mince through and made my white bechamel sauce, and I assembled this beautiful lasagna, only for the children to say they hated it, which was horrible of them. To be fair, Joanie doesn't really like lasagna, but I kidded myself that it would be different this time. 'Look,'

I said, 'I know you don't like lasagna, but Mummy's cooking it from scratch. I think you'll like it.'

But no, she's just not keen on lasagna, which blows my mind, because it's just flat pasta with bolognese, and she loves spaghetti bolognese. What's the difference? Mind you, I did put ricotta cheese, mozzarella, boiled egg and peas in it, as well, which is the traditional Sicilian way. Oh well, Marc and I enjoyed it, and I've got two portions of it in the freezer – and I'll know for next time.

When I'm in the mood for cooking but just can't decide what to make, I remind myself that a meal is like a comedy or a drama. Whatever the comedy, it's the same characters every time, dressed up in a different way. And there are only seven basic dramatic plots – a hero may defeat a monster, set out on a quest, go from rags to riches, transform through suffering, make a fatal mistake, triumph happily over adversity or go on a journey of discovery. It's just a question of reinventing a storyline and writing it in a different manner. What's all this got to do with cooking? Well, it's the same with food: same ingredients, different ways of creating and combining. All it needs is a situation, inspiration and a good ending. Apart from when you've slaved away for a couple hours making a fancy Sicilian lasagna, only for your children to turn their noses up at it! We've all been there, right?

Songs That Remind Me of My Brother David
- 'I Believe in Miracles' – The Jackson Sisters
- '(Fallin' Like) Dominoes' – Donald Byrd
- 'Our House' – Madness
- 'Sex & Drugs & Rock & Roll' – Ian Dury
- 'This Charming Man' – The Smiths

Songs That Remind Me of My Brother Tony
- 'The Whole Of The Moon' – The Waterboys
- 'Don't You (Forget About Me)' – Simple Minds
- 'Shake It Off' – Taylor Swift
- 'Wish You Were Here' – Pink Floyd
- 'With Or Without You' – U2

In Search of Time

Tracking time is a complex business. We take calendars for granted, but humans have been trying to find an accurate way to organise time ever since the Stone Age.

There are four types of calendars: lunar, solar, lunisolar and seasonal. It took hundreds of years of staring at the sky to decide that a day lasts as long as it takes the Earth to rotate on its axis; a month is the length of the moon's rotation around the Earth; and a year is the time it takes the Earth to orbit the sun (or vice versa, as was originally assumed). Eventually, stargazers were able to predict the seasons and know when to plant and harvest crops. Bronze Age people tracked time by arranging stones or making markings on sticks. Today's calendars come with pictures of cats, flowers, models and celebrities with their tops off.

Calendars quickly became incredibly complicated because the movements of the Earth, the sun, the moon and all the planets vary slightly and it's not easy to calculate a system to synchronise them. Early astronomers in the Near East kept having to bung in a month here and there, so that their equivalent of Christmas didn't come early.

The early Romans had a calendar that charted ten lunar months, from March to December, and followed the harvest. They sensibly didn't bother counting the drabbest winter months (I'm with them on that one) until a certain King Pompilius came along and named them January and February. He didn't think about the knock-on effect of that though and forgot to adjust the other months, so September means 'seventh month' when it is in fact the ninth month of the year. October, November and December are still quite wrongly called the 'eighth', 'ninth' and 'tenth' months, but it's probably a bit late to be changing them now.

The Aztec and Mayan cultures in Mesoamerica had several calendars. One marked a 260-day year that had no link with the planets or the seasons, so the theory is that it was calculated to last the length of human pregnancy, from the first missed period up to birth. Another calendar had 365 days in line with the solar year. Every fifty-two years, these two calendars synchronised and everybody had a party.

The solar year lasts 365 days, five hours and forty-eight minutes. When Julius Caesar seized power in Rome in 49 BCE, he introduced a 365-day solar calendar with an extra day cunningly inserted every four years to make up for the extra hours. He named the calendar, and the month of July, after himself – and who can blame him? I quite like the sound of Natuary!

After all that careful planning, though, it turned out that Caesar had put in the wrong number of leap years, causing the seasons to start slipping. So, in 1582 Pope Gregory XIII modified the Julian calendar – and promptly named it after himself. These guys!

The Gregorian calendar is now the most widely used in civil life around the world. There are only four countries that haven't adopted it: Afghanistan, Iran, Ethiopia and Nepal. Many other countries have their own traditional calendars, and so in Java they're in the 1950s and in Korea they're in the 4350s, while Bangladesh languishes in the 1430s. Imagine that!

Our house ran like clockwork when I was growing up. Mealtimes, bedtime and playtime were all predictable. I feel like the patterns you've been brought up with are important because life's very different now. Time seems different these days, in that there is no time. We're not cooking at half five or all sitting down together to mark the end of the workday. You'd love to be, but it's just not possible in today's world. Our hours are extended, work's extended, the kids have activities after school and want to spend time with their friends. We all want these perfect family lives, but with the way the world is, I think we're going to have to redefine what that means to us.

In our house, the kids will eat early on a school day. Sometimes Joanie will eat at five, then Eliza wants to eat at half-six, seven, and then Marc and I eat. I try to be around as much as possible for the children; I'll be with them when they get home, but I won't eat with them at five because I'm not really hungry at that time. I'll cook and then I'll probably sit down for my meal once Joanie goes to bed, around half eight. In the summer months, I'll sometimes just pick: a bit of cheese or pâté and cherry tomatoes, and a piece of chicken. Who wants a pie in July? In the winter, once the kids are in bed, I'll cook a nice pasta, or steak and wedges for Marc and me, maybe watch a bit of telly, or look at booking guests for *Life with Nat*. At the same time, I'm also checking my business WhatsApp for messages from listeners on the pod, or checking Instagram and replying to questions there, or looking at an email. It never ends, and I feel like I never switch off. When I get really busy, it sometimes feels like my brain is hurting from thinking so much. So, I'm really trying to make an effort to put my phone down of an evening, to leave it in the kitchen and not go near it. I think you really need to be strict with yourself and just switch off sometimes and read a magazine or supplements from the weekend newspapers.

The clockwork operation of my childhood home still whirrs within me, and it's one of the reasons I started to think about leaving *EastEnders*, to give our family more routine and predictability. I knew that, in order to do it, I needed more control over my schedule and working life, something that's impossible when you're acting in a soap.

My listeners on the pod love that I'm doing things for the first time. I've had so many messages from people saying, 'You've inspired me. I'm stuck in a job that I don't like, but listening to you, I might change my career and start something new.'

It's that Monday feeling . . .

Monday Art Class

Monday's atmosphere can be quite elusive. I love art and art history, but if I commissioned a painter to capture the essence of a Monday, I'm not sure who I'd choose to do it. My favourite painter is Caravaggio, but I don't think I would choose him. His paintings always look like he created them in a wild trance in the middle of a Saturday night, after a debauched party. Maybe Michelangelo's *The Creation of Adam* in the Sistine Chapel in Rome is nearer to capturing that Monday mood. *Wake up, ping! Life begins*. And that applies to all the other days of the week, too.

Never forget: each day is a fresh start and we're all so lucky to be here.

Chapter Two

Bank Holiday Monday

If it's not a wash-out and the sun is shining, the May Day Bank Holiday can be a really happy day. Dawn comes early; winter darkness has shrunk away. There's a freshness in the air, a blossomy sense of summer promise. Now is the time to dig out your picnic things and head off to the seaside.

Go early, though – you don't want to get stuck eating your sarnies in a ten-mile tailback on the motorway! It's no good sitting in a stuffy, stationary car longing for a cool dip in a river that's two gridlocked junctions away. It's the very definition of bank holiday madness. If I know it's going to be sunny, I'll get everyone in the car no later than 7 a.m. to beat the rush.

We used to have thirty-three public holidays in the UK every year, based around saint's days and religious feasts. Imagine that? Good times. But then in 1843, the Bank of England cut them to four: Good Friday, 1 May, 1 November and Christmas Day.

People went about feeling disgruntled about this, until a politician named Sir John Lubbock introduced the 1871

Bank Holidays Act, with four new holidays: Easter Monday, Whit Monday, the first Monday in August and Boxing Day. The public were so grateful that, for a while, they called them St Lubbock's Days.

They've switched the bank holidays around a bit, but a century and a half later, we still have eight bank holidays a year. Some people still think it's not enough though. India has twenty-one! Only Mexico is below us, with a measly seven. I'd like a few more – and why not? Maybe one in March and another in June . . . or how about putting one in each of the months that don't already have one?

In 2011, Parliament debated moving the May Day Bank Holiday to October, to spread the days out more evenly, but it came to nothing, and I'm personally glad of that because I had my first date with Marc on May Day. Leave it where it is, please! It's a very special day for me.

There is an element of 'what if?' in every couple's story. 'If I hadn't made that call/missed that bus/got caught in the rain/taken that flight/swerved that party . . . I would never have met you!'

Marc and I always say that we wouldn't be together if it wasn't for David Bowden, a cameraman at *EastEnders*. He's our 'what if'. I've worked with David since I was ten and started on the show; Marc knew David's daughter through a group of girls at his school in Kent.

Marc wanted to be a cameraman growing up, so when he found out that his friend's dad worked at *EastEnders*, he gave her a letter enquiring about work experience: 'Could you give this to your dad?' David read Marc's letter and arranged to bring him along to Elstree one day, to see how everything worked.

Marc tells a story about his first ever day on a set: 'We were waiting around for an actor . . . and then YOU walked in, saying, "Sorry, I'm late!"'

It's weird, because I usually do everything I can to get somewhere on time. I really, really hate being late, I do everything I can to avoid it happening, and it annoys me in other people, as well. I don't mind it when it can't be helped; it's unapologetic lateness I dislike, like someone just not being ready on time. They're ambling around at home and they're going to be forty minutes late, for no reason, and everyone else just has to hang around waiting for them. I don't understand it. So, it's kind of ironic that Marc's first impression of me was that I was really unprofessional and running late. It's all a bit blurry now, but I think I might have overslept . . .

I don't remember meeting Marc that day, but years later, when I went back to *EastEnders* after a long break, there he was. 'Who's the gorgeous cameraman?' I asked Patsy Palmer, in my first week back.

She knows me so well that she just grinned. 'Like him, do you?'

'He looks nice,' I said.

She linked her arm in mine. 'Come on, I'll introduce you.' Marc and I instantly hit it off. He's got such a lovely, open, friendly way about him. There was no side to him. What you saw was what you got. He was just . . . Marc.

We started to have a little chat in between scenes. At one point he mentioned the day he came to *EastEnders* for work experience, and everyone was waiting around for me to show up.

'No, that can't have been me! I'm never late,' I insisted.

An excited tension sprang up between us whenever I was in a scene that he was filming. It was all quite nice, but then I realised I didn't know his name, and I wanted to look him up online. In the end, I cornered one of the runners, and said, 'Can you find out his name for me, please?'

'It's Mark Humphreys.'

So, there I was scrambling on Facebook looking for an M-a-r-k Humphreys, but couldn't find a match, because he's Marc with a C. Eventually, someone dug out the correct spelling for me and I finally found him on Facebook.

I made the first move:

Hi! Really enjoyed chatting with you at work, I wrote. *I just thought we could link up here – and it would be nice to maybe have a chat?* I put my mobile number at the end of the message.

Immediately, he phoned me, which I thought was really daring, even though I'd given him my number – it's not really the done thing to call someone, is it? You'd think it'd just be a few messages here and there on Facebook, but he phoned me straight away and we chatted for about an hour – a bit about work, where he lived and where I lived. It was a really nice, fun conversation, and that was the beginning of it all.

Now that I've known Marc for eleven years, I completely

understand why he phoned me straight away, because he does like a good old chat on the phone with his friends, even today, when everyone else is sending texts and leaving voicenotes.

About two weeks in, Marc asked me what I was doing over the May Day Bank Holiday, which was coming up at the end of the week.

'I quite fancy going to Whitstable,' I said.

I told him about how I used to go for a ride out to get fish and chips in Whitstable with Mum and Dad on a Sunday.

'Yeah, I really like it there,' he said.

'Do you want to go?' I asked him.

'That would be great,' he said, and then we carried on talking for another hour.

The plan was that I would drive and pick him up from his house on the way to the coast. I'd never done that on a date before; it was a first for me, and in a funny way, everything else that happened on that day felt like a first too. I was so excited on the drive down. We'd already been talking for hours on the phone in the morning, and now we were off to Whitstable together for the afternoon.

The sun was out when we arrived and we went for a wander. There was a May Day parade and a carnival that day, with lots of bands and music everywhere, and people marching through the streets. Everything felt heightened: the colours, the music – it was how love feels. We sat and had a drink at the Old Neptune pub right on the front by the sea; it was the pub where I knew Mum and Dad used to go when they were younger, and it seemed a fitting place to be falling in love.

At the end of the day, I thought, 'This is special. We really get on.'

Meeting Marc was a turning point in my life. I was thirty, which is quite a pivotal age, and I suddenly met this man and thought, 'I need to shape up a bit here, because he's really nice. I'd like to be with him.'

It's not like I was some badly-behaved nightmare before I met Marc, but he brought out the best in me and made me want to be the best version of myself. I hadn't felt that before, and maybe that's because Marc seemed different from anyone else I'd ever met. He has a really dry sense of humour; he's funny, intelligent and interesting, and even after all these years, we've never run out of things to talk about. We discovered quite a few coincidences as we talked too, including the fact that we both had older parents. There were little things too and they all added up to the feeling that, somehow, we were meant to be together. Sometimes you just know.

Before long, I realised that things were getting serious. It was weird; something clicked and there was an immediate feeling of, 'Ah, I get it now.'

It probably isn't very romantic to say so, but in a way, I suppose falling in love isn't much different to thinking, 'I really want to do my own podcast.' It's a passion in you, and you think, 'This is really good, and I want to do everything I possibly can to make it work.'

Everything takes effort. It upsets me if Marc doesn't feel as happy as I think he should be; if he's not happy, I'm not happy, and vice versa. If we're both happy, we're content, and so I do what I can to increase his happiness. It's the same with the girls. You are only as happy as your unhappiest child, and so you try to make sure they are as happy as they can be.

Marc gave up quite a lot for me. He moved away from where he lived in Kent and came to live with me in Hertfordshire, an hour and a half away. That was a big sacrifice. He took on quite a lot, too, because I already had Eliza, who was three when we met, and later my dad, who was getting older and was unwell at times. Marc immediately fell in love with Eliza, and it took no time at all before he was treating her like she was his own daughter. He also got on brilliantly with my dad and was happy when Dad came to live with us. Since then, we've had Joanie together and we've gained so much. But we've also gone through loss together too: Marc lost his father, and I lost mine, and we were there for each other throughout those times. All these things bring you closer together.

Being in a blended family can have its ups and downs, but I've been extremely lucky that Marc and Eliza hit it off from day one. Eliza has always seen Marc as her dad, and it means the world to me. I know that, for some people, it can feel really hard to meet someone new when you've got a child, because they're your number one, but I think you have to trust that the right person will be willing to accept that, and in time, hopefully develop their own connection and relationship with your child. Families come in all different shapes and sizes, but I really do believe that the most important thing for kids is to know that they're loved.

Eliza and Marc's song was 'Daddy Cool' by Boney M. Marc would wind her up and say it was written especially for her when she was little, and she believed him! It's so lovely that they have such a good relationship.

Marc proposed in the October after we met. It was all very quick, but somehow, we just knew. It felt as if it was meant to be. We also started talking about having a child together, and very soon I was pregnant, just under a year after Marc and I got together. It was the same getting pregnant with Eliza – it happened easily after deciding to go ahead and try. I know how some people can have so much difficulty getting pregnant, and I feel really lucky that I never experienced that. Both of my pregnancies with the girls were very different though. My relationship with Eliza's birth father had been fraught from the beginning and went on to be continuously stressful, whereas with Joanie I was in a much happier place, which made the whole thing so much easier.

When we were having Joanie, people used to say to Marc, 'How exciting! You're going to be a parent for the first time.'

It upset him and made him cross: 'I'm already a parent,' he'd say.

I used to have to cut in and say, 'People aren't being rude. They're just talking about you having your first baby.'

But he just wouldn't have it. His mum, Jacqui, who's like my second mum, felt the same way. When people said to her, 'You're going to be a grandmother for the first time,' she'd get really annoyed.

'Actually, I've got Eliza. She's my first grandchild.'

It's been lovely that everything worked out as it did. I'm sure we'll have some turbulence along the line and questions will come up for Eliza, but we'll deal with it. I've always been a great believer that friends are the family you choose. Blood or not blood, if you love somebody, they are your family, aren't they? After all, let's be honest – there are people with sisters whose best friends mean more to them, and I think that's okay.

Mine and Marc's Songs
- 'Pick Up the Pieces' – Average White Band
- 'Get Lucky' – Daft Punk ft. Pharrell Williams & Nile Rodgers
- 'The Diary of Horace Wimp' – ELO
- 'Kodachrome' – Paul Simon
- 'Linger' – The Cranberries

I am not someone who believes one way or another in the supernatural. I didn't have an opinion on ghosts growing up and didn't have any remotely supernatural experiences. But about two weeks after I'd got together with Marc, I was in bed asleep one night and I woke up to this baking hot sensation; it felt like I'd just got off an aeroplane in a hot country.

I opened my eyes and saw my mum sitting at the end of my bed, smiling at me. I blinked and blinked again. She wasn't floating like a ghost or an apparition; she was very real and there were folds in the duvet around where she was sitting. Petrified, I reached out to my bedside light and switched it on. In an instant, the warmth was gone and so was Mum.

It was about two o'clock in the morning, but I immediately picked up the phone and rang Marc and said, 'The weirdest thing has just happened to me.'

That fleeting moment was over very quickly, but I won't ever forget that warmth and Mum's smile. I absolutely believe it was Mum showing me that she was happy for me that I'd met Marc. But after that, I became more scared of being on my own at night than I had been before. It was an amazing experience but it wasn't a comfort, and I didn't ever want it to happen again. Even now, I'll lie in bed and think of it.

People say, 'You had your head in the clouds after meeting Marc, so maybe it didn't actually happen; maybe it was a dream.'

Maybe they're right and it was just a very vivid dream, who knows? Mum had passed away eleven years earlier, but I felt her presence and I saw her. I've never had an experience like it since.

Eleven years after that first date in Whitstable, I still find Marc endlessly interesting. It's great – I can talk to him for hours about all sorts. I can't imagine being with someone who bored me to tears; I just couldn't do it.

I look forward to those nights when it's me and Marc at home and I don't have work to do. We still have the hubbub to get through: he'll be doing emails on his laptop, I'll be getting dinner ready, and then we get Joanie to bed, and Eliza's up for a bit. It's like a nice deep breath when, at last, we can sit down together and have a glass of wine and talk – and we never run out of things to talk about.

I know loads of people who don't really do that evening thing – they don't even sit in the same room because one's watching the football and the other is in bed watching a box set. It's fine if that works for you, but it was ingrained in me from Mum and Dad to be together in the evenings, and I've taken that on with Marc.

Much as Marc and I like an evening in together, we do love a date night too. We try and make the effort to go out together, even if it's only once a month. We've been really busy recently, but it's important to say, 'We're getting a babysitter and we are going out,' even if it's just down to the local pub and then for a meal. It feels like a real treat to have a bit of food that neither of us has had to cook and get to enjoy a drink and to chat away to each other. Lately, we've even ventured so far as to have a night in a hotel. As a mother, I truly believe that you never fully switch off at home – there's always that feeling that the door might open because someone's had a bad dream, and to be able to feel sexy and passionate is so important!

Funny story: one year, in Marc's Christmas stocking, I wrapped up some door wedges, which puzzled the kids but delighted Marc!

In a relationship, you need to find time for each other, especially when you have children, because children become everything. Remember that you're a partnership and one day, those children won't be around. You're bringing them up to fly the nest, and then you're going to be left with somebody who you live with, who perhaps you don't know. So, you need to stay in tune with your partner, and make sure that you grow together, as well as bringing up your children.

I don't feel the need to be with someone for the sake of just being with someone, and I've never been afraid of being single. Sadly, I think there are a lot of people who stay in relationships they're not happy with for financial reasons, because they can't afford to go it alone. Other people stay because they feel like they can't get out for controlling reasons, which is a horrible situation to be in. But I'm none of these. I'm completely self-sufficient. I don't need to be with Marc; I *want* to be with him. So that's quite empowering, because I want to spend time with him. I still get excited about a night with Marc, even after eleven years together.

People will say, 'You're so boring. Are you phoning him again? Are you texting again? So sad.'

They're winding me up, but I don't care. It's what I want to do, and if I still feel that way after eleven years, how lucky am I? Of course, all relationships have their ups and downs. You have your arguments and your insecurities with each other: 'Are you all right? Do you still find me attractive? Do you still love me? You've been really quiet. You've not met anyone else, have you?'

I'm terrible for projecting my insecurities sometimes. I'll watch a Louis Theroux documentary about sex work in London, say, and when Marc comes home, I'll be saying,

'Why are you late?' and I'll be really moody with him. He's got no idea what's brought it on, and of course, he's just been caught late at work, not sneaking off to see a sex worker, but your brain can do terrible things.

We get bombarded with bad stuff, which is why, sometimes, you have to make the effort to switch off from everything. Phones, the telly – just turn it all off! When you're sitting in a room with a glass of wine and you're having a chat without any distractions, human to human, it really brings you closer together and makes you feel happier, glowing and more centred.

You can get that feeling from a night with a really good friend, too. It can be totally joyous to catch up with a mate and put the world to rights. It's just as good, but without the sex. That said though, sex is good for you! Afterwards you think, 'Why don't I do that more often? It's great. I must remember it and keep doing it all the time. Oh, but I'm so tired!' And it is genuine tiredness.

That's where a man and a woman are completely different, I think: if as a woman, you offer it up, it doesn't matter what's going on, he wants to do it. But it's definitely not the same the other way around!

*

A bank holiday means you can make a long weekend of it – or, if you plan it, a longer break. My favourite places to go on holiday are Italy, Ireland and Cornwall – they are all places where I feel a sense of belonging.

'You feel like you could move to wherever you are on holiday,' people say, but I don't think that's true.

I'm not overly well travelled, but I have been to Australia, Greece, Spain, New York and quite a few other places, and in none of them do I ever feel that same deep-rooted sense that I belong there. Why? What's the connection? On my dad's side, my great grandfather was from Ireland and my great grandmother was from Naples in Italy, so maybe it's a cellular memory. But, if that's the case, then I think I must have some Cornish ancestors because I get the same feeling when I'm in Cornwall looking out at the sunset over the sea.

When I booked to go abroad to Greece last year, Joanie cried her eyes out. It was as if I'd told her that she was being punished for something, and I couldn't understand it. 'What on earth is wrong?' I asked.

'I just want to go to Cornwall, Mummy.'

Even for the children, Cornwall is a really special place. It's our family place. We stay near Padstow. Or Padstein, as they call it, because Rick Stein is everywhere with his hotel and restaurant and café and whatnot. We'll be going abroad again this summer, but it's back to Cornwall at Easter. Part of the fun when we go to Cornwall is getting in the car with your pyjamas on, because it's such a long drive. Even Eliza, now at fifteen, really looks forward to being woken up at 3 a.m. and getting in the car. Everything gets you in that holiday mode, from the music we play, to the girls falling asleep and waking up to find that we're in Cornwall in time for breakfast. No matter what you can afford or where you go, I really do believe that it's those family memories that are everything. There's a lot of pressure with social media and whatnot, but I really do believe that you don't need to spend a lot to have a really brilliant time. And we're lucky that we've got such a beautiful country where you can just get in the car or on the train and go somewhere amazing. You don't have to feel bad if you're not getting on a plane this year, because whatever you do will be special.

When bank holidays were made official, the railway companies started putting on specially scheduled 'Picnic Trains', so that city dwellers could enjoy a day out in the countryside or at the coast. Imagine the excitement of the kids inside the carriages of those trains, getting to escape from the soot and grime of the city on a sunny day, armed with their fishing nets, cockling equipment, buckets and spades, parasols, blankets, picnic hampers and parents.

Trains have a special place in our family. When Eliza was nearly four, all of us went on one of our first family trips together, taking a steam train along the beautiful Bluebell Railway route in Sussex. We went with Marc's family: his mum and dad and brother, so it was quite a big deal, fairly early on in our relationship. I'm a people person and so I was excited about meeting them, rather than nervous, and we had a lovely day out. It was very easy, as it always has been with Marc's family: his mum Jacqui took to Eliza immediately; she and Marc's dad Roger, who we've since sadly lost, took Eliza on as a granddaughter right from the start. Since that first train ride, we've also been to Tenterden, and my favourite,

Romney Hythe and Dymchurch in Kent, but I'll always hold that first trip on the Bluebell Railway in my heart.

Marc has always been interested in steam trains: he fired up his first engine at the age of ten; years later, he started to build his own chassis in his spare time, and some of his train friends helped finish it. It's a ride-on train with a seven and a quarter gauge engine, the type you get in garden centres, and now it runs through a fantastic sculpture garden and woods over near West Horndon. It's called Barnards Miniature Railway and it's in a really beautiful setting – the perfect place for a picnic.

I'm not a railway geek by any stretch of the imagination, but I don't mind going along with him. Eliza has grown out of it, but Joanie still enjoys it. Poor Marc is going to have two teenage girls soon, but I'll still go with him to the trains.

It's a lovely thing to do. There's something about steam that is just very nostalgic – you see it in all the old films, and of course, it was such a huge part of Britain back in the day. I always feel like we're being transported back in time to a more innocent era, or at least to a time when life was a lot simpler, and people mostly travelled by train instead of car.

It's funny that we can be nostalgic for a time that we didn't live through. I find it with fairgrounds, as well. We've been a couple of times to the Hollycombe Victorian Steam Fair in Liphook in Hampshire, where there's an old-fashioned carousel and Victorian penny machines. It's amazing, like being in Mary Poppins.

Whenever we go on a day trip, I always like to take a picnic, but if we haven't been for a while, I have to stop and think: at the end of our last picnic, what are the mistakes I swore not to make again?

Picnic Necessities
- Two tins of G&T or a nice, cold bottle of wine
- A bottle opener
- A wine cooler
- Reusable plastic glasses, plates and bowls
- A picnic blanket with a waterproof underside, or a waterproof sheet to put under your blanket
- Two bin bags, one for rubbish and the other for dirty plates and bowls
- Two knives
- Kitchen roll or wipes
- Sunscreen
- Plasters and antiseptic spray
- Soothing cream for bites and stings
- A beach umbrella if there aren't going to be any trees for shade

I always have a perfect vision of what a picnic should be in my mind, but it doesn't always turn out that way, does it? I remember me and my dear friend, Julia, one of my besties, taking the kids on an idyllic summer's day to Hartham Common Park. Julia has two girls too – her eldest was born on the same day as Eliza and her youngest is around the same age as Joanie. We were all set for a heavenly day enjoying the sunshine and relaxing outside. We spread out our blankets and started to lay out our sandwiches and salads. 'Oh, this is fantastic,' we said. 'What a brilliant idea. The weather couldn't be better . . .' and all the rest of it.

Along came a wasp. Then another. We swatted them away; they came back. Soon there was a swarm of wasps buzzing everywhere.

The kids needed a wee. The sandwiches were warm. A dog came over and tried to eat a sausage. We couldn't help laughing as we hastily packed everything away. It was just one of those days when you say, 'Well, that's life, isn't it?' Best-laid plans, and all that.

It can be even worse on the beach, where everything's covered in sand. Even so, I'll carry on having picnics until I'm old and grey, because sometimes they do actually live up to the dream – and then there's nothing in this world that is better to do on a lovely summer's day.

How to Keep Wasps Away

- Wear light colours, but not bright colours – you don't want them to think you're a flower
- Put out a bowl of cucumber or put cucumber peel around the edge of your blanket – wasps hate it. Garlic, too
- Light citronella candles or sit near a eucalyptus tree
- Pack your food in Tupperware boxes and cover it when you're not eating. (As if . . .)
- Capture the first wasp you see, as it may be a scout on the look-out for food. To stop it flying back to the nest

to report your trove of picnic goodies to the rest of the guys, pop it in an upside-down jar or glass until you leave

- Hang a wasps-nest-shaped paper lantern on a nearby branch as a security decoy. They'll think twice about messing with another colony

May Day and the August bank holiday top and tail the summer. By the time that last long weekend comes along at the end of the summer, the days have a beautiful golden slant. This is one of the last chances you'll have to indulge your fantasy that the summer will last forever. How could the temperature ever drop? You just can't imagine it getting dark at four, or having to put on a coat, hat, scarf and gloves on top of two jumpers and a thermal top just to pop to the shop for some milk. 'Not going to happen,' you think, as you lie back, relax and feel the sun on your face for a few final moments.

Enjoy.

Chapter Three

New Year's Day

Apart from the fact it was my lovely dad's birthday, I've never been a fan of New Year's. I'm a massive Christmas head, so the fact that January is about to arrive and it's all over just makes me feel a bit depressed.

I'm also quite a stubborn person. I don't like being told what to do, especially when it's a demand – 'You must do this. You must do that!' Whether it be trying a food or learning something new, I need to do it at my own pace.

Probably because of this, I usually ignore New Year's resolutions. A lot of people have said to me, 'Are you doing dry January?' Then they tell me all about how they've gone on a diet, or that they're stopping this or stopping that. Personally, I think January is the worst month to give up anything. The parties are over, the sparkly decorations are down, the weather is miserable. You have nothing to comfort you, and then you're expected to be giving things up on top of all that!

January for me is more about *hygge* – the Danish and Norwegian idea of feeling contented and homely. In winter, hygge is a time of bedding down, of being cosy – lighting candles, slowing down, wrapping up in a soft blanket or a lovely scarf. Some linguists say that it comes from the Old Norse word for hug, and that just about sums it up: whether you're feeling hygge at home, or out with friends, it's like being wrapped in a warm hug. And who doesn't want a warm hug?

For me, it's getting in from a day out, putting on your most comfy clothes and hunkering down. You can't beat that, can you? Be it an old nightie, or a great big pair of tracksuit bottoms and your favourite old jumper that's got a hole in it, or maybe even a lovely new set of pyjamas or loungewear that you've been given at Christmas. Marc bought me a beautiful White Company pair of pyjamas that I hang on to. They're covered in black and white stars, and God, they're old now, but I still wear them because I love them. Eliza still has her favourite teddy and childhood blanket that she'll put on the end of the bed, and I think it's the same thing. It doesn't matter what age you are, we all love that feeling of comfort.

Lighting is also really important. I love the dark in the winter, so I'll often have a little lamp on in the lounge and then lots of candles. Even in the kitchen, sometimes I'll just have the cooker hood light on and candles – although I'm hearing more and more now that all these lovely, scented candles are bad for us and release toxins into the air, which is a fact that I'm choosing to ignore for now!

We used to have an open fire when we lived in our old house in Broxbourne, and there was nothing better than when

Marc got home and lit the fire. Unfortunately, this house doesn't have a fire, and it is something we miss. But maybe we'll go the other way and get one of those modern gas fires that stand in the centre of the room with a big flue up into the ceiling, who knows?

I love a comforting bowl of hot soup in winter, but only at lunch time. I can't just have a soup for dinner, much as it would be lovely to be one of those people who eat like mice and have a little bowl of soup and call it a day. It's not enough for my lot, but stews and bolognese always go down well in the winter; chicken stew and dumplings is a meal the kids always like, just as I did as a kid, and I do toad in the hole, those sorts of dinners.

At midnight on 31 December, Old Father Time traditionally hands timekeeping duties to the Baby New Year, and there's a sense of a renewal of the cycle of life. Why does it happen on this particular day? January is named after Janus, the Roman god of beginnings, but why would the middle of winter be seen as a time of beginning, when nature seems at its deadest and most dormant? Why not March, when spring arrives, and green shoots appear? That would make much more sense to me.

The start of a new year is celebrated by different cultures at different times all over the world. The Chinese New Year falls either in January or February and is associated with spring; the Iranian and Balinese New Years are in March; the Bengali New Year is in April; the Zulu people celebrate New

Year in July; the Ethiopian New Year falls in September; and the Inuit mark their New Year on 24 December.

During the Middle Ages, church authorities in Europe tried switching New Year's Day to religious dates in March, April, September and December, but none of them ever caught on. So the calendar went back to day one on 1 January, ten days after the winter solstice, when the days start getting longer.

To be fair, you don't hear much about Old Father Time these days beyond sci-fi novels, comics and heavy metal songs. I wonder why. Has someone replaced him? He is based on Chronos, the ancient Greek personification of time, and the Baby New Year is aligned with Dionysus, the god of wine and festivities. Maybe that's why we drink champagne on New Year's Eve? Or maybe it's to steel ourselves as we gear up to start work after the Christmas season.

Possibly the worst New Year's Eve I ever had was the Millennium. I was sixteen at the time and the Millennium was meant to be a really big deal, although to me it seemed more of an excuse for a big party than the dawning of a new era. Anyway, some friends and I thought it'd be amazing to go to the Thames to see the fireworks. The reality was different: we stood in the rain, with nothing to drink because we couldn't get anything, dying for a wee, freezing cold, and feeling miserable. Awful. It didn't bode well for future New Year's celebrations, and I never really went anywhere after that; for the most part, it's always been family, either round to theirs or having them over to us.

In my twenties, when *EastEnders* was at the peak of popularity, I used to get invited to really fun things. One year, I got to go to Jools Holland's *Hootenanny*. Even though it's a celebration of New Year's Eve, it's actually filmed three months earlier, in October, which might be disappointing to some people, but seemed pretty normal to me because I'd been filming Christmas scenes in the autumn for twelve years at *EastEnders*. The only difference was, at *Hootenanny*, I was being myself, not playing a part. But I love a celebration, whenever it is, and this was absolutely amazing – Paul Weller was performing, and Lily Allen, Amy Winehouse, The Kooks – so many great artists. I got to sit on a table with the pop artist, Peter Blake, and it was very relaxed; we were listening to the music and enjoying the evening. I told him how much I liked art, and he told me all about creating an album cover for The Beatles. I felt so lucky to be there. My life isn't always glitz and glamour, and that evening was one I'll never forget. Someone suggested I do my own version one day and call it *Hootenatty* – you never know, maybe one day I will!

In the years since, I've usually been at home with Marc, the girls and my dad, because he'd always come over and stay for New Year's before he moved in and lived with us. We would put Jools Holland on the telly, have some champagne and sing 'Happy Birthday' to Dad at midnight, by which time the girls would be long asleep. Then we'd usually finish our drinks and go to bed. Not very wild, but it was never boring either. I'd still be dancing round the living room as we said goodnight.

My dad was born on New Year's Day, 1937, two years before the beginning of the Second World War. I used to love sitting and listening to him talk about his experience of life during the Blitz. One day, when he was about five, he came home to find that his house had been flattened by a bomb. Suddenly, he had no home. After that, like many of London's kids, he was evacuated out of London. But unlike most of them, he went with his siblings and mum and dad. They all moved to Lincolnshire, where they lived next to a farm and had an amazing time. Dad told me about how he used to climb fences, nick apples and help the farmer with various chores. Every day he walked five miles to school and back again. He was only five or six, but he remembered all of it so vividly, which isn't surprising. For a boy from wartime London, the rolling green hills and massive skies of Lincolnshire would have been like another world. Honestly, I think he would have been happy to stay there and not come back to the city at all.

With a lot of people, you mention the Second World War and they understand that it was a terrible thing, but they may not know the layers and intricate little details of what it was really like to live through it. I feel like I'm lucky enough to have that understanding from my dad, who was that much older and passed his memories on to me. After his house was destroyed by a bomb, Daddy knew that anything could happen any time – I think the generation who grew up during the war were made of harder stuff and didn't let much get to them. Dad spoke about the war often. It had such an impact on his life and I think we maybe don't always take that into account as much as we should with that generation

Because New Year's Day was Dad's birthday, I'd always cook us all a nice meal to celebrate: usually a roast dinner. Although you're sick of roasts by the first of January, a piece of beef can be nice, or ham, egg and chips, which Dad loved. In fact, the last meal anyone ever made him was ham, egg and chips, cooked by Ellia, my niece, so that very simple dish feels really special when I look back now.

Back in the day, before we had the kids running around pestering us, Dad and I would have a game of Scrabble whilst dinner was cooking because that was our game. We were quite well matched most of the time, although in later years, the grumpier he got, the more I let him win. We'd always put some music on, listen to a bit of Frank Sinatra, and he'd have a whiskey or two and I'd have a couple of wines. It was lovely.

Just like my mum with my Nanny Liz, I enjoyed caring for my dad as he got older. I tend to be much better at taking care of other people than I am at taking care of myself. It's terrible, but I'm not very good at going to the doctor's or for health check-ups. I know you should go, and as they say, prevention is better than cure, but even so, I always have a little voice in my head that goes, 'If it ain't broke, don't fix it.'

I think the reason I feel funny about going to the doctor's goes back to my dad, who had a lot of health problems, mainly to do with his heart. When I was ten, he had to have a triple heart bypass – the operation was obviously a wake-up call, because he said, 'Right, okay, I've got a ten-year-old daughter . . . time to change things.'

All the cholesterol was cut out, the full English breakfasts. The fags went too – he could get through forty cigarettes by ten o'clock in the morning when he was at the paper shop, but as soon as he was told he needed a heart operation, he chucked them in the bin and never smoked again. He was a real all-or-nothing person.

That operation changed everything, and once he'd recovered, Dad pottered along and had a lovely life. When Mum was alive, she really looked after him and made sure he ate a healthy diet. After Mum passed, though, Dad moved to Lincolnshire to be near his brother, who was living there at the time. It was also a return to where he'd been evacuated in the war and that was a big part of it as well, because he had always wanted to go back there and relive those happy memories. It must have been a shock to the system for him to suddenly be living alone, because he'd never had to cook in his life – my mum did it all for him, once they were married. That's how it was back then. But, instead of being lazy and eating ready meals and takeaways, he learned how to cook, and making dinner became a part of his day. He built it into his daily routine: he'd play golf and then come home and start preparing his meal at four o'clock, with a little drink. He'd have Dover sole with new potatoes and loads of veg, or a salmon fillet, or rainbow trout, or steak. He always liked plain, English food, and that never changed.

Eventually, Dad moved back to Broxbourne to be nearer

to me and my brothers and lived in a retirement flat for a few years. He was in and out of hospital with different health problems, but he still liked to cook his own dinner every day. In 2018, I moved him in with me and Marc, so that I could keep an eye on him and take him to his appointments more easily. Joanie was eighteen months old then, Eliza was coming up to eight, and I decided we needed to start looking for somewhere that would give us all a bit more space. Marc was fine about living on top of each other – he welcomed Dad with open arms – but I wanted Dad to have his own annexe.

I looked at a few places, but none of them felt right for us. Then one day, our estate agent called me up and said, 'I think I've got something for you.' I drove to a nearby village, where she showed me around this beautiful house that was actually two houses in one, with a front door adjoining them. We couldn't really afford it, but when I saw it for the first time, I remember thinking, 'This is it! We have to buy it. I'm just going to make it happen, no ifs or buts.'

We had to move mountains to finance it, but we did it, and I'm so glad we did, because it meant that we could all live our own lives while I kept an eye on Dad – and he kept an eye on me, as well! It was the perfect arrangement, really, and I felt so lucky to have him near me. Everything about the house was brilliant, in fact – and still is – from its peaceful setting in a quiet village next to a farm to its lovely spacious rooms and garden. Having a nice big garden is wonderful, especially in summer, and Marc really loves it – in part because he can grow his tomatoes and chillis and other veg, but mainly because he's built a train track around the rockery and a tunnel for his engines through the garden shed. It's a magical sight – something that he and the younger kids in the family will be enjoying for years to come – and we've also now got Joanie's little fairy garden out the back and a lovely area for entertaining when the weather's good, as well.

When I look back at Dad moving in with us, it was something we just had to do. There was no question about it. I just knew in my gut that it was the right thing to do, and Marc went with it, and so did the girls. Throughout my life, it feels as if things have happened for a reason. I don't question much; I just go with it. It was hard when Dad was in and out of hospital while Joanie was very little, but Jacqui, Marc's mum, helped me out a lot. Everyone mucked in and it worked. Of course, there were some stresses over not having time to yourself. Marc and I would be in the lounge and Dad's room would be next door and, while he wouldn't be able to hear you asking him if he wanted a cup of tea, he managed to make out every word of even the most whispered conversation we had in the lounge!

Three years after he moved in, Dad was still cooking his own meals and washing himself. He was 84 and really self-sufficient; although he was sleeping quite a lot, he was free of dementia and Alzheimer's. But one day, while we were watching the golf together, I noticed that his ankles were quite badly swollen. 'They look a bit funny,' I said. 'I think we'd better get those checked out with the nurse.'

Dad used to get so annoyed when I did something like that,

and he'd accuse me of fussing. 'Leave me alone!' he'd scold and try to change the subject.

'No, Dad, I think we should get it checked out,' I said firmly.

The doctor came, and before I knew it, we were in hospital. They wanted to do an ultrasound, check for clots, and look at Dad's heart. He had been diagnosed with an aneurysm at the beginning of the Covid-19 pandemic, but because of all the lockdown restrictions, it hadn't been checked or tracked for months. We knew it was growing, but we didn't know how big it was, or whereabouts in his body.

As we sat and waited for the ultrasound results, I was bracing myself to hear bad news, but I was certain it wouldn't be anything we couldn't fix. Dad was still playing golf, still cooking his own food. Then, a doctor came over and said, in front of Dad, 'Your father's aneurysm is a triple A aneurysm. It could burst at any minute.'

I couldn't take in what he was saying. It was one of those moments where everything just changes in an instant. I looked at Dad. He was pale and shaking. It was so scary. He was already on blood thinners and lots of other medications, but I'd never imagined that we'd hear such devastating news.

'We'll get him admitted now,' the doctor said.

'What for?' I asked. 'What are you going to do to help him?'

'There's nothing we can do because he's too unfit to operate on. We've been through all of this before.'

'So, I'll take him home,' I said firmly.

Thankfully, they allowed it, but quite frankly, they didn't

have a choice. I knew I just wanted to make Dad as comfortable as possible and for him to be surrounded by those that loved him.

It was April. I remember driving back into the village feeling petrified, but desperate to keep it together for Dad. I remember saying to him, 'Well, we'll just forget that. If we hadn't come today, we wouldn't have known.'

Back at home, I phoned my brothers, sobbing, and told them what the doctors had said.

My brothers couldn't take in what I was saying. It all felt utterly surreal, and it was heartbreaking to have to explain what it meant.

'He hasn't got long. Everyone needs to come and see him.' They rushed to be by his side, but I think we were all in a state of shock. To them, Dad seemed to be the same as when they'd last seen him.

In my mind, I can't help but think that, if we hadn't gone to the hospital that night, he might not have gone downhill as quickly as he did. Hearing those words from the doctor sent him into such a downward spiral, and I wish the doctor had thought before he spoke, pulling me aside and telling me the news, rather than saying it in front of Dad in such an abrupt and unfeeling way. The mind is a powerful thing, and I think my dad heard the doctor's words and thought, 'That's that, then.'

Those last few days were spent in warm April sunshine. Dad would come outside and sit on his bench; I knew he was worried about what the doctor had told him, but we never really spoke about it. Instead, we'd sit together and have a cup of tea and just savour each other's company.

Gradually, the reality of Dad's prognosis seemed to sink in, as we all realised we needed to make the most of every minute we had left together. My nephew, Dominic, came over and watched some golf with dad, which was lovely. 'Are you going home?' I asked him, in the late afternoon.

'Actually, I'm going to stay a few more hours,' he said, and the two of them spent a lovely evening together, perhaps not realising that it would be the last nice evening they'd share.

Everyone ended up coming to see Dad. His best friend, Gary, came, and that day was the last time Dad was able to sit in the garden. All the family came over and we had two or three days where Dad was in bed, with nurses coming in, and he wasn't speaking anymore.

A brilliant woman, 'Linda the carer', as she's still listed in my phone contacts, was a godsend. She'd pop in and see Dad when I was at work, do a bit of cleaning, keep him company, give him a cup of tea. Linda was like an angel; she had looked after the elderly quite a bit, so she had enough experience to guide us through that time. She wouldn't leave us until I said, 'Go home! You must go home.' So, she went and came back when we needed her.

It was sad, but in some ways, they were also the most beautiful few days I think we've ever had as family. People were cooking and drinking and chatting, and then we'd go into the room and sit around Dad's bed and talk, and there would be quiet moments. It was very peaceful and serene, and looking back, it was perfect, actually – I can't think of a better way to go out of this world than being surrounded by those who love you.

I was there with Dad when he died. It was a Saturday morning. His brother George arrived from Newcastle. George was eighty, and I'd said, 'You don't have to come down.' But he wanted to, so he drove all that way with his wife, my Auntie Eleanor.

I thought, 'Well, that'll be that, then, because he's waited for his brother.'

I'd not had a shower for a few days because I'd been sat with Dad, so I went and showered. Then I realised I'd not really eaten much, either. My nephew, James, said, 'What can I do, Auntie?'

'I'd like a really large gin and tonic, and I'd like a ham sandwich with lots of butter on it,' I told him gratefully. It's so hard to remember to look after yourself when you're so focused on looking after someone else, but I'm so lucky to have such a caring family around me who can take care of me in those moments when I forget to.

About half an hour later, Dad left us. It was quite peaceful. I knew he was going, and me and my brother, Tony, were by his side. I rubbed Dad's arm and told him that I loved him and that it would all be okay.

'Linda the carer' was there as well, and it was lovely having someone there who had experience of being with people in their final moments.

That was that, really. I remember coming out of the room

and there was a lot of crying, as well as some relief and sadness. Mainly, I remember feeling absolutely exhausted. Everyone around me was drinking and chatting and crying, but I just curled up on the sofa, and I slept. I slept all night long. I felt like I'd done what I had to do; it was quite animalistic. I'd been in survival mode for about a week at this point, going through the worst emotions possible, because I knew I was going to lose him. Now, there was nothing more I could do. The worst had happened, and it was over.

Looking back, though, it really was a perfect experience, if you can call death that. The fact that his passing was so peaceful, and so filled with love, made it easier to accept losing Dad. Let's not forget, as he always used to say, 'There's only two certainties in this life: death and taxes.'

I think of that often, and it reminds me that we have to enjoy life as much as we can because none of us really know how long we have left, or how much time we'll have with our loved ones. Dad left us in 2021, and I still miss him very much.

Chapter Four

Tuesday

I like a Tuesday. In my mind, it's a calm day. You've got over the beginning of the week; you're not jumping ahead and desperately looking forward to the weekend. It's a settling-in day. Does that make Tuesday forgettable? Quietly nestled between Monday and Wednesday, is it slightly overshadowed by them, a bit of a non-day?

My Joanie was born on a Tuesday in August 2016, so it's a memorable day for me. On a global scale, Tuesday's rating is a mixed bag, and it seems to mean different things to different people. In Greece it's known as 'the third day' and is viewed as unlucky because bad luck comes in threes. In Spain, where Tuesday is 'Martes', after Mars, the Roman god of war, it's traditionally a bad day for starting anything important. That seems to be the same in Hinduism too, but for astrological reasons.

In Judaism, though, Tuesday is a great day when good things happen. In Japan, it's a day of fire, named after the red-hot planet Mars, and a lucky day. D-Day was a Tuesday, a crucial day. And for party people worldwide living for the weekend, Tuesday means you've got through Monday and life is looking up!

> ### Accept or Resist?
> When something goes wrong, and then something else goes wrong, and you groan and think, *'It's going to be one of those days!'* are you setting yourself up for more problems?
>
> If you actively challenge that mindset and say, 'Things can only get better from here,' can you reverse the direction of the day? Or should you just go with the flow, accept that, yes, it is one of those days, and lean into the blows?
>
> There's a middle way, I think: keep hoping.

For me, Tuesday has always been one of my red-letter days because when I joined the cast of *EastEnders* in 1993, the show was being broadcast twice a week, on Tuesdays and Thursdays, and we always watched it on telly.

I was lucky to get the part of Sonia Jackson. Probably many little girls could have done what I did, but you have to be in the right place at the right time to get a break, and sometimes that does just come down to pure luck. In my case, that luck meant being at one of Anna Scher's acting classes in Islington the day that *EastEnders* came looking to cast kids for a new family that was being introduced to the show in late 1993 and early 1994.

I was eight when I started going to Anna's classes. The fact that I started going at all was pure chance – it only came about because my mate was on her way there one Friday night and her mum popped into ours, and said, 'Do you want to come, too, Nat?' Like I say, pure luck. Saying that, though, it was luck combined with a love of getting up and performing, if only in the middle of the lounge when people were round, or up at the hospital with my nana. Knowing this, my mate's mum probably thought Anna's classes would be right up my street, and she was spot on.

Anna's theatre and workshop was in Penton Street, Islington, about a twenty-minute walk from our house in Dagmar Terrace. It was an old building – there was nothing special about it, but it was Anna's, and Anna was extraordinary. Small-framed and dynamic, with a smile that went from ear-to-ear, she was a powerhouse: she was very strict, but intelligent, well read and well travelled – and her classes were wonderful. Before starting at Anna's, I'd done a couple of school plays and was developing a knack for comic timing, but I was a nervous performer, and Anna gave me confidence. I remember my hand shaking like a leaf while I was reading poetry in front of the class, but with Anna, it was okay to be scared, so long as you pushed through and did it anyway.

I still get nervous about live performance, which might surprise people to know, given how long I've been acting. It's something I joke about, but it's actually terrifying. Sometimes it helps me to think back to those days when I was a bundle of nerves in class, hands trembling, voice wavering. 'If I could get through it then,' I think, 'I can get through it now.' Over the years, I've done a lot of live telly, including the scenes where Sonia is giving birth in the rubble of the Queen Vic pub for the fortieth anniversary episode of *EastEnders*, and it doesn't get any easier at all. I have such admiration for the likes of Ant and Dec, Rylan and Claudia Winkleman. They make it look so effortless, but I know that live television really is a skill.

I loved going to Anna's, and after a couple of years, I graduated to the young professionals' class on a Saturday afternoon, where people of all ages, races and backgrounds got together and did improvisational work, read poetry and sang songs. Anna's was an equal, inclusive space; as well as teaching us acting skills, it also provided an education in the school of life. My love of poetry began there; she had a 'Winston board' that had a new word on it every week, inspired by Winston Churchill's habit of learning a new word from the dictionary every day. Even more importantly, I respected Anna and respected her rules because I loved what I was doing. I just wish there was more of that now. We're all so different, and for kids to have to sit in a classroom each week doing exactly the same thing as the person next to them isn't easy. Going to Anna's taught me how important it is to find your niche in life; to discover a passion. When you find that, you also discover that you want to learn and do well; to be respectful and kind to people, and to show the teacher that you're learning and that you love it.

Anna was great at nurturing talent, and she helped people like Kathy Burke, Daniel Kaluuya, Linda Robson and Dexter Fletcher on their way.

Casting directors would come to Anna's and sit at the back of the theatre and watch the class. We'd line up on stage and say our names and give some basic information about ourselves: 'My name is Natalie Cassidy. I live in Islington and my favourite colour is green.' Then we'd do our little improvisations, and they would pick a few people to invite to an audition.

I'd been at Anna's a couple of years when I was chosen to try out for *EastEnders* up at BBC Elstree Studios. They were looking for a small, blonde, waif-like girl, apparently, and, of course, I was the complete opposite of that, but I was a funny little thing, and they seemed to like my character. Suddenly, before I knew what was happening, bang: I was cast as Sonia. I had no idea how much that moment would change the course of my life forever.

I was at school the day the producers called my mum to say I'd got the part. She told my brothers before she told me, and they couldn't believe it. Television and viewing habits have changed over the last thirty years, but *EastEnders* was regularly being watched by fifteen million viewers back in the Nineties, so it was a really big deal. My brother Tony remembers sitting in McDonalds after he heard the news, Big Mac in hand, staring out of the window in shock, thinking, 'My little sister is going to be in *EastEnders!*' It must have felt so surreal.

I remember Mummy picking me up from primary school in the afternoon and saying, 'Guess what? You got it!'

Getting the role of Sonia meant that Mum became my chaperone and started taking me up to Elstree for rehearsals and filming. Nanny Liz hadn't long passed, and Mum was missing her badly. On top of that, she and my dad had been through a huge amount of worry earlier in the year when Dad had undergone his triple heart bypass operation. Mum had cared for him throughout, and now that he was better, it was a nice change for her to be taking me up to Elstree. She got a small fee for chaperoning me – it wasn't a lot, maybe £35 a day, just a bit of pocket money for her – but it was a chance for her to venture out of Islington and make new connections. She made a wonderful friend in Debbie Alexandrou, whose son was James Alexandrou, the actor playing Martin Fowler, and the one who gets Sonia pregnant when she's fifteen.

Dad went back to work after his heart surgery, but he had more help now, and wasn't doing such long days, so he often walked me to school on his way to the paper shop. If he was going to work earlier, Mum took me, and she always picked me up at ten past three on the dot, without fail. I used to love seeing her at the school gates, the same way that Joanie loves it when I'm able to pick her up at the end of the school day. It's one of those big memories from childhood, isn't it? Mum and I used to walk past the sweet shop where Mum and Dad met, and I'd usually get to go in for a treat. One of those lovely links in the chain of life.

I spent my first days up at Elstree during the gloomy, cold October of 1993. Despite the grim weather, though, I absolutely loved it, even though I was just popping in and out at the start because union rules meant I could only work forty days a year. I wasn't there out of any desperate want or need for work – as I say, it was pure luck – but once I got the part, it was down to me to grow my character and keep my role.

Looking back, I was so incredibly fortunate to have some of the best actors in the business showing me the ropes at such a young age. They taught me the importance of professionalism and hard work, values that I carry with me to this day.

It's ridiculous to think of the amazing women I grew up with on set: Dame Barbara Windsor, Wendy Richards MBE, June Brown OBE, Pam St Clement and Lindsey Coulson. We spent so much time together at work that they almost became like a second family, and these were strong, matriarchal women. I'm not someone who has ever been impressed by celebrity, but I know how lucky I was to be acting alongside such a stellar cast. Patsy Palmer and I had both come through Anna's, and the two of us were like sisters growing up together. Patsy lives in Malibu now, and I may not see her for months on end, but when I do, we click back in straight away. It's the same with Dean Gaffney, who played Sonia's brother. Dean is one of those people I may not talk to for a few months, but if he rings, I pick up the phone and it's like talking to a family member.

Being at *EastEnders*, it really did feel like we were a collective; a tight-knit group. Of course, I was a child, and I had a lot of respect for the adults, but I was listening to the likes of Barbara, June, Pam and Wendy chatting about the TV jobs they'd done and the theatre they'd done, or just having a moan, and I was soaking up every word like a little sponge.

They would be stern with me on set – and I don't think it's a bad thing to be stern with someone. It does feel like times have changed since then, though – I feel I'd probably get called up if I were to say to a child actor what June used to say to me: 'Speak up, dear! I can't hear you. You're mumbling, dear, you're mumbling.'

You can't say anything like that anymore, but she didn't mean it in a bad way, and the lesson she was trying to convey has never left me: when you're acting, you have to be heard. The first eight or nine years I was there was like an acting apprenticeship. I was at the *EastEnders* school of life, constantly learning how to be on time, how to know your lines and how to be a professional.

June was a constant in my life right up until she passed. Our relationship truly became a friendship over the years, despite the differences in age and the fact that she'd known me since I was a mumbling little girl; we used to drink red wine together and we even went on holiday to Malta together a couple of times. We'd stay in a hotel and do a Q&A evening for some of the guests in return for the holiday. The rest of the time, we sat by the pool, reading books and eating nice food.

June was brilliant fun to spend time with. She had a wicked sense of humour and used to chat to everybody. She was flamboyant and she could be flirtatious, but underneath all that, she also had a shy side. She had a lot of love for her family, and she always had time for her fans, who she valued hugely. I wonder if that has rubbed off on me. She made friends with quite a few of her fans and used to talk to them on the phone on a Sunday afternoon. She'd really take the time to go through all her fan mail personally and reply to people, which I think is lovely.

June was very honest with me, right from the beginning. One thing she said that I'll never, ever forget – and I love it so much: 'Remember, every line in every scene is a song. Never be monotone. Think about the pauses. Think about how you're saying something: if it's up, or if it's down, and whether or not you need to slow it down or pace it up.'

That has stuck with me. Do I practice it all the time? Probably not, because we worked so hard at *EastEnders* and sometimes there wasn't time. But I'd try. Another thing June stressed was the importance of listening while you're acting: 'You can know your lines, but if you're not listening to me, you'll never get it right,' she'd say. 'Half of acting is listening to the other person or people in the scene and reacting.'

With Barbara Windsor, it was all about being on time and knowing your lines back to front. She was the ultimate professional. I remember her whizzing into work and just wowing everybody. Everything about Barbara was infectious – her laugh, her smile, her warmth – and she had this perfect little shape; she was just great and it means the world to me that I have the pleasure of calling her then-husband Scott Mitchell my agent and friend.

Lindsey Coulson, who played Carol Jackson, Sonia's mum, used to coach me on set with nuggets of wisdom like, 'Take your time, Nat. Don't panic. You don't need to rush it.'

Sometimes you can get on a set and feel quite babbly, because you're thinking, 'Oh no, this scene is all me.' You can end up burbling.

'Just breathe,' Lindsey would say. 'Don't just say the line.

Think about what you're saying. Why are you saying the line? What is the intention behind the line?'

One surprising downside of starting to act so young is that my memory isn't brilliant – it is very short term, which I really think is because of using certain muscles more. For thirty-one years, from the age of ten, I trained my memory to learn lines and then immediately chuck them away afterwards. I'm no neuroscientist, but I've got a feeling that in the process, I've also thrown away some of my core memory, which is a little bit disturbing and a bit sad too. Ultimately, though, I remember the things that really matter, and maybe other memories of life will return as I start to lose that habit – if I ever do.

Lindsey came to my fortieth birthday party a couple of years ago. She laughed as she hugged me, and said, 'I will never forget you as a young girl standing on set. The director would be chatting to everyone, and you'd say, "Excuse me, so I was thinking, what do you think if I . . . ?"

'It was hilarious,' she said, 'because you were only ten or eleven, and you'd be talking to the director like we would. Nothing wrong with it, but you didn't see it often in people of your age. You had no fear. You'd say, "Actually, I don't know if I'd be sitting here." Or "I'm not sure – would you mind if I do it like this? Because I don't think Sonia would look at Bianca like that . . ."'

The technicalities of TV acting can be very difficult because you have three or four cameras on a set at a time. Although I was only ten when I started playing Sonia, a character who is two years younger than I am, I was lucky to have an instinctive sense of where to be in a scene. It sounds very simple but, believe me, I see people in their fifties who still can't do it now.

When I look back now, I think I was very fortunate to have these women as my work colleagues – and they were also my good friends.

In the UK, Tuesday is named after Tiw, or Tyr, the Anglo-Saxon god of war and law. According to Norse mythology, Tyr was a single combat hero who had his hand bitten off by a wolf. Legend also has it that his nan hated him – and she had nine hundred heads. Nightmare!

Imagine being little toddler Tyr and having your nan come over to babysit! Nine hundred pairs of eyes staring at you as she serves you up a bowl of goblin entrails.

You, having to say, 'This is delicious, Nan! Honest, it is.'

Nine hundred mouths saying, 'Good, then you'll be wanting seconds!'

People sometimes ask me if I would encourage my kids to go into this industry, and it's a tricky one to answer. Eliza was fabulous when she played Miss Trunchbull in the school production of *Matilda*. She has a lovely singing voice as well – not that I tell her, because I don't want to get her head too big – and I think she would really like to go into acting and performing.

It's very difficult for me to say, 'Oh, you don't want to do that. It's such a precarious career,' because she'll turn around and say, 'Why not? Look at you!'

'But I've been lucky. Very, very lucky,' I'll remind her.

'I know, but I might be lucky.'

I don't want to put a negative spin on it, but I know so many people who want to be in the entertainment industry and haven't had the breaks. It really is so hard to be out of work as an actor or singer, and there's a lot of rejection and competition.

'If you want to perform, go and study law,' I tell Eliza, 'because barristers are all actors.' I once did a play with Jemma Redgrave, who was married to a barrister at the time, and I remember hearing her talk about the performative side of arguing a case in court. As a barrister, you're standing up and telling a story in a persuasive manner, which is acting! But you have to work hard if you want to become a lawyer, and a good work ethic is a huge thing for me.

Above all else, though, I just want Eliza to be happy, whether she works as a train driver or a film star.

*

I started my education at Hanover Primary, a lovely little school in the middle of Islington. It was very 'Jeremy Corbyn' in that we didn't wear uniform, and we called the teachers by their first names. My favourite teacher, Arabella, was red-haired, cool and bohemian; the head, Cynthia, was like a much-nicer-but-still-scary Miss Trunchbull. She used to carry her little pug, Angel, around the school with her.

After primary, I went to Islington Green Comprehensive

up the road. Why did Mum and Dad choose that particular school for their little chicken? Because I only had to cross one road to get there! Honestly, I'm not joking. (Actually, Daddy always called me a little squirt.) Never mind the open days and school brochures – that was their sole reason for sending me to Islington Green.

It really was a different time back then, when you tended to go to the nearest school to your house. I don't think there were the same pressures as there are now to go somewhere Ofsted 'Outstanding' or 'Good'. These days, it's still the haves and the have-nots, but it's by postcode, and whether you can afford to live somewhere that's got a good school nearby. One of the best state schools in the country is in St Albans and you can't get a house in the catchment area for less than 1.5 million pounds. Imagine!

Islington Green School wasn't a bad place, but it was quite rough around the edges. Most of the time, I just got on with it. I was in the second set for Maths, and the teacher used to wear flip-flops with her long toenails curling over the edges. That was a vision on a morning in assembly!

I had some nice teachers, and I did well in year seven and year eight, but by year nine, I'd fallen in with the crowd that didn't want to learn, and I started thinking, 'If you can't beat them, join them.' I wouldn't say it was bad crowd, but we'd bunk off occasionally and be down the canal smoking, that sort of stuff.

Now that I've got a teenager of my own, I worry about the impacts of peer pressure, especially in a world of social media, when they're getting it from all angles. I'm constantly reminding Eliza, 'Don't bother about the popular kids. Don't go there. Just do some good work.'

At the same time, though, I try and reassure myself by thinking, 'She'll be okay. I didn't turn out a bad person.'

I do want Eliza to do well at school, though. I encourage her to get all her homework done at the weekend and to revise hard for the next exams.

'But Mum, they're irrelevant,' she says.

I can't really argue with her – I think there are far too many exams for kids these days, and honestly, I don't think kids should be doing exams through their most hormonal years, when they're experiencing all these changes with friendship groups, relationships and how they feel about their body. I think it's completely bonkers that they have to sit exams and do mocks when they're fifteen and sixteen. I'm never going to say it, but what I really want to say is, 'You're right, it's all irrelevant, all of it!'

I don't tell her all that, of course, apart from to say, 'But it's practice, darling. All the revision you're doing now stands you in good stead for future exams.'

Maybe it seems like a contradictory viewpoint that I don't think exams are the most important thing in the world, because I'm paying for Eliza's education. I know a lot of people would say, 'Why are you spending x amount a year if you're not really on board with the curriculum?'

I went to state school for primary and secondary school, and I've sent both girls to the local village primary school. But when it came to secondary education for Eliza, I really wanted her to have what I didn't have, even though it was a tough choice and it's not always easy for me to do, financially.

When people find out that I've sent her to private school, they'll often say things like, 'I bet you want to see that money back.'

I find that attitude really puzzling, and I'll ask. 'What are you talking about?'

'Well, if you're spending all that money, you obviously want her to go on to a job that pays.'

I can honestly say, it's not about that for me. I chose to send her there for the smaller class sizes, the brilliant sports facilities, and the extra well-being and pastoral care her school provides.

My brother Tony talks about the 'knife edge' of parenting teens. Once they get to a certain age, you have to let them go out and have a bit more independence, but which way will they go? Tony had a lovely childhood friend who used to play out down near the flats near us back in the late Seventies. One day, this friend was offered heroin and that was it. He became a heroin addict and then a crackhead and a thief. It can happen that quick – which is why it's such a knife edge.

I think there are even more risks for going in the wrong direction if you're a kid wanting to impress people who are doing stupid stuff. For me, it was more a case of trying to placate my classmates, who were really pissed off that I got to have days off school to go to work. They didn't like the fact that I could be off on a Monday and a Wednesday having a nice time at *EastEnders*. When I got back to school it was always, 'Why are you allowed to miss school and we're not?'

For my part, I was thrilled when I reached thirteen and the number of days I could work doubled to eighty a year. It caused further resentment and jealousy among my classmates, though. I was bullied for it in secondary school and I also got comments and jibes about what I looked like, because I was a bit on the larger side. My way of coping and trying to deflect the negativity was to act like a bit of an idiot and make people laugh. I've got a very thick skin and just got on with it. Now, every success I have is a finger up to all the bullies. But although I was at Islington Green less and less as my days spent on the *EastEnders* set increased, I really did always like doing my schoolwork. I loved English and loved writing – though I'd never have imagined then that one day I'd get to do something like this and get to write an actual book! What a dream come true. I left school at sixteen, but I've long dreamt of going back to studying one day. I like the idea of having to read books and write essays.

As luck would have it, I'm currently working on a BBC documentary about social care, and I'm going to college for the first time, in my forties. I'm doing a Level 3 NVQ course for real – it really isn't just for the telly – so I'm doing coursework and assignments, and I've got an exam coming up in about six months. It's been years since I've sat an exam! I'm in a classroom with loads of Gen Zs, who are sixteen and seventeen years old, and some of them are young carers, whilst others have had experience of being in the care system. I've also been going on different placements, including dementia wards and care homes with older folk, so I'm getting to meet such a diverse range of people from all walks of life. One day, I was up at the Royal British Legion with some veteran soldiers with PTSD doing a mental health awareness course, which was a real eye-opener. The course ranges from early years all the way through to end of life, but I have a particular interest in end of life and elder care because of my experiences looking after my dad. I'm thinking that if I do this NVQ at Level 3, I may then want to have a deeper dig into elder care, or think about doing another course at a later stage. I've been waking up in the night thinking, *Maybe we could find a space and I could open a care home nearby*. Who knows what the future might hold! It's full-on, and it's a world away from life on *EastEnders*, but I'm finding it really humbling and lovely to be learning new things – and it just goes to show that it's never too late to go back into education, or to try something new.

Indie Music

When I was twelve, I got into Oasis in a major way. I really and truly fell in love; I was completely obsessed with them. I was part of the fan club; I wore the T-shirts and I had the dog chains; the fan magazine arrived every couple of weeks, and I used to walk around all day at school with a CD player and headphones in my ears, listening to *(What's the Story) Morning Glory?* on a loop. In fact, I remember standing in a park in Islington with my CD Walkman, playing it over and over again and crying because the boy I liked at school didn't like me back. He wasn't much to look at, and that's not me being unkind – it's just that no one else liked him, really. Still, he was super intelligent, and I had the biggest crush on him. It was my first experience of that awful pain, that terrible feeling you have the first time you really like someone, and they don't like you back. Listening to Oasis got me through it and my crush soon transferred to Liam Gallagher.

Call me an Britpop hypocrite, but I loved Blur as well. I never hated anybody – I listened to Pulp, Supergrass, Echobelly, The Stone Roses and Paul Weller. I got into The Beatles through Oasis too – they were always saying, 'We're going to be bigger than The Beatles.' It made me wonder, 'Who are these Beatles?' even though I'd obviously heard of them. So, off I went and listened to them, and I loved them too.

Oasis will always have a place in my heart. I have all the B sides on a beautiful vinyl album that Marc bought me for my birthday; I still have an Oasis T-shirt; I even have Liam Gallagher's tambourine in the loft!

I was lucky enough to see Oasis back in the early 2000s, and was actually at their last gig at Wembley before they split, so when the new tour was announced, I was ecstatic. I was thinking of turning up before the gig and saying, 'Liam needs his tambourine back. I'm here with the band.' There also aren't many people who have been on *The Great British Sewing Bee* and made a Liam Gallagher parka, you know. Lots of people on Instagram said I should get a ticket just on the strength of that. In the end, I couldn't even face trying to queue for tickets. I would have been too heartbroken to not get them, so I decided to sit tight and trust that I'd manage to get there somehow. Then, for my birthday, I opened a card from Marc's sister Jen. She'd handed it over so casually, so when I read the note inside saying I had tickets for Oasis, I couldn't believe it. It is quite possibly the best present anyone has ever given me, and I don't think I'll ever be able to thank her enough.

It was the best gig I've ever been to – even better than seeing them back in the '00s. Every moment of the day was just a joy. You could really tell that every single human you bumped into was sharing the emotion and excitement of seeing the brothers back together again. I cried when Liam and Noel headed onstage but they really did give us two truly brilliant hours of nostalgia and love. I sang along to every single song and it was one of the best days of my life. I'll never, ever forget it. Oasis forever.

I left school at sixteen because I loved every minute of working at *EastEnders* and couldn't imagine anything else being more interesting or fun. Being on set was a brilliant learning experience. Back in those days, you didn't have the same stringency in place that you have now. Children in television workplaces are no longer allowed to sit around the adults like they used to. They have their own room; they're brought on to set when they're needed and then they're whisked off again. That's all well and good, but I learned practically everything I know about acting, as well as lots of valuable life lessons, not only from being on set with my fellow actors, but spending time in those green rooms with the adults too.

My first proper kiss was at work, whilst on set, interestingly enough. Not the most romantic thing in the world! You're working with someone, and it says in the script that you kiss them, so that's what you do. Sonia had her first snog with a lovely boy called Enrique, an Italian exchange student. It was Sonia's first snog, and it was my first proper kiss, as well, and if I'm honest, it was a bit like a wet weekend . . . ! I'd also kissed a boy at primary school while playing The Scrunchy Game in the playground, when I smacked my lips onto a young kid after he took my hairband out and ran off with it. It was some kind of mad kiss-chase game, so also not the most romantic! But after I had my big crush at secondary school, I got so busy with work that I wasn't overly bothered about boys and dating. I just went out and had a good time.

I love a nap. When you're asleep, your body is replenishing itself, re-nourishing and regenerating all the cells, so if I can squeeze a nap in, I will. I have no guilt about it. It can be two o'clock in the afternoon, and I can sleep for five minutes, thirty minutes or two hours.

If I'm at home, feeling tired, and I look at the clock and it's a quarter to three, and I need to pick Joanie up from school, I can still go to sleep. I can set my alarm for fifteen minutes and immediately go into a deep sleep. Two minutes after I wake up, I'm feeling energised and ready to go and pick her up.

My skill for napping has been honed and facilitated by all the years at *EastEnders*, where our dressing rooms had little beds. Now that I've left, I'm not having as many naps now, and it makes me very cross, although towards the end, I shared a room with Patsy Palmer and I had to wean myself off a bit because we were constantly chatting. I think naps are very important. I don't have to be tired or feeling overworked to have a nap. It's not about mood. I can have a nap at five o'clock for an hour and still go to bed in the evening.

Marc's mum Jacqui bought me a book about sleep, and I really took it seriously. Everything I read in it resonated. We talk about European countries and how Mediterranean people live longer; we talk about the Mediterranean diet, and the benefits of a warm climate, but people rarely mention the famous after-lunch siesta. I think it's one of the secrets to a longer life.

It was busy and chaotic in the Jackson household, where Sonia lived – everyone in and out, rushing around. Life on Albert Square was a world away from my home life with Mum and Dad, where life was quieter and more regimented, maybe because they were older parents and liked their peace and quiet. At home, we always had a family Sunday lunch, and the days ran like clockwork. Saying that, I'd have mates over and they'd stay the night, and my niece Maria was always staying with us, so it wasn't a house where no one was allowed in. I always wanted company, and even today I don't like to be on my own much. People say it's linked with being the only child in the house, because my brothers were almost grown up when I arrived, but I think it's just the way I am. These days, I enjoy the quiet space of the daytime when the kids are at school and Marc's at work, but I still don't like being alone after dark.

When I started on *EastEnders*, I'm not really sure how much I connected with the character of Sonia. I don't remember ever thinking, 'How am I going to do this?' I just came in and played her as a member of this chaotic family. Sonia was a lovely little thing and had a lot of character. I was especially lucky early on with the scenes I got to do with Robbie Jackson, played by Dean Gaffney – like the time Robbie was making Sonia get drunk by forcing whisky on her. Then, of course, she started learning to play the trumpet, and people seemed to love that, even though she was terrible at it. All these years later, I'm still being given trumpet-themed things as presents – I can't get away from it!

As the years went by, Sonia grew with me. It's impossible not to bring a part of your own self into a character that you're playing every day. As the years passed and she fell in love with Jamie Mitchell, and he died, and different people came and went, and people that she really loved left the show, I realised that in layering and building Sonia's history, I knew more about who she was and how she felt than almost anyone. Once I'd been on the show for a while, I found myself in the position of getting a script and just knowing that Sonia wouldn't do what had been written, because of this or that that she'd experienced. It's a real privilege being able to play such an active role in shaping your character, and to really have those insights and understanding of why they do the things they do.

Having played Sonia since I was a child, my perspective is different from someone who comes to the show in their late twenties and has to build their character without having lived the backstory. They have to do a lot of work, of thinking, 'What has this character done before? Where have they been?' But I didn't need to do that. I'd grown up on set, and Sonia grew with me.

Funnily enough, there are definitely some real similarities between me and Sonia. I like to make people happy, and I've always been a carer, and Sonia is quite a caring person too; she's a nurse and she's very sweet. We've both spent a lot of time in hospitals as well. Life almost writes itself sometimes, doesn't it?

I always had a clear idea of how Sonia should look. She doesn't have a sense of fashion and that's a conscious choice I've made. She's downtrodden and has always worn quite drab and dreary clothes because she doesn't have lots of money and fashion isn't on her radar. She doesn't care; she puts on clothes because she needs to, and that's fine. I think there are a lot of people like Sonia. It makes her real, and it isn't glamorised.

It's similar to the choice Barbara Windsor made when she decided Peggy Mitchell would be glamorous, and the way Jessie Wallace made Kat Slater so iconic with the leopard print, the red lips and the high heels. In Jessie's case, I'm sure it was born out of a collaboration with the wardrobe department, but she's kept it up – she knows her look, and it's strong. I've gone completely the other way, but that's who Sonia is. I'm protective of what she stands for. If you were to change her look and glam her up, she wouldn't be Sonia.

You can recognise an iconic character from a silhouette. You see it with Kat, and with Pat Butcher, because of her earrings, and Dot Cotton, with her hair. Interestingly, people say that you can tell Sonia from her outline: the trumpet in her early years, and the big, hooded coat that she wore towards the end.

Sonia also never wore a lot of make-up and always had her hair pulled back in a velvet black scrunchie. 'That's too nice for Sonia,' I'd say to the wardrobe people, when they brought out certain outfits. I ended up being quite strict about it. 'I'd wear that, so Sonia can't.' That's how me and Sonia are different – I love a nice top, a pretty dress; getting glammed up. Don't get me wrong, I can do casual with the best of them, and very often I don't wear a full face of make-up or have my hair styled, but I always knew instinctively what was and wasn't right for Sonia's character.

Sonia would wear certain trainers, and a top with a long cardigan, which is an idea I took from Carol Jackson, Sonia's mum. Carol liked her cardi, and I imagine Sonia would be influenced by her mum's dress sense, although Sonia's sister Bianca went completely the other way, with a silver puffer jacket. Bianca's look was kind of mad, and none of it really matched, but it was perfect for her character, and it's become quite iconic and stylish now. If you go into Primark, there are loads of silver and gold jackets – funny how these things come back around. Somehow, I don't think Sonia's outfits are ever going to come round and be trendy.

The day I left *EastEnders*, someone asked, 'Is there anything you'd like from Sonia's rail?'

It really made me laugh. I said, 'No, thank you. You can tie it all up and put it away.'

It felt like an important part of separating myself from Sonia after so many years. The next day I dyed my hair, which was something I could never do while I was on the show, because Sonia wouldn't have ever dyed her hair. I did quite a few things to consciously and metaphorically leave her behind, and I found the whole thing really liberating. It felt like a sign that I was stepping into life as Nat, rather than squeezing the real me in around my role at work.

My earnings from *EastEnders* went into an account and my parents made sure I wasn't able to spend much of it until I was eighteen. Other than that, Mum and Dad didn't give me a lot of guidance regarding saving or investing. Their attitude to money was simple: when you have it, spend it. Dad worked really hard and spoiled us all. It was Wendy Richard who told me to start a pension at eighteen, which I did, and I'll forever be grateful to her. Steve McFadden, who plays Phil Mitchell in *EastEnders* and is a brilliant actor to work alongside, has also given me some great advice over the years and has always looked after me, on set and off. He suggested that I invest in a property, which was invaluable advice as well. I bought a flat just along the road from my mum and dad in Broxbourne, which was the right thing to do, although it still took me a few years to learn how to manage my finances.

I can't help but spend money. People may say, 'That sounds a bit careless,' but I don't like holding on to it. Life is too short!

However, there's a difference between being gener-ous and being stupid, and I have become more sensible about money matters – doing my taxes properly and so on, although it's only in the last two or three years that I've begun to understand how it all works. If you're not used to it and haven't got a business mind, it's quite difficult, but I know what I'm doing now.

You need to be able to manage money when you're a mum. For me, having a good accountant to help me keep on top of everything is really important. I always had quite stuffy, older accountants – nothing wrong with that – but now a school mum friend does my accounts. 'Charlotte, explain it to me like I'm a two-year-old,' I say, and she doesn't mind doing exactly that. She'll tell me precisely what to do, and I understand her.

I used to completely shut off with those kinds of things. I really hate having to do admin, but over time, I am getting much better. It clears your head a little to keep on top of things. There aren't any little goblins whispering in your ear in the middle of the night saying, 'You haven't done this and you haven't paid that.' It gives you peace of mind.

Money is such a big issue, in every area of life. It's all very well for me to sit here and talk about how it can be tricky to pay for a nanny or school fees, but at least I can afford them – and I do work hard. But I'm very conscious that some people don't know when their next pound is coming in to put food on the table. It's something I'm lucky enough to have never experienced, but I do have so much empathy for those people. I remember discussing on a podcast how much freedom children should or could have, and listeners were calling in with stories about their kids running around fields and jumping into each other's gardens. It struck me how much circumstances play a part, and I made sure I spoke up for the people who live in inner-city London, in a flat with a couple of kids, and how it must be difficult knowing their kids are going out into the city. I don't live in cloud cuckoo land and I know how lucky I am. I always try to put myself in other people's shoes.

Money means different things to different people. I find that the more generous you are, the more money comes to you. I'm also well aware that money doesn't make you happy, but in most circumstances, it can certainly help make life easier. I say to the girls: 'You've got to work hard, because you do need money to live well.'

Pancake Day

Once a year, people across the world eat, drink and make merry on Shrove Tuesday, a religious holiday that non-religious people also celebrate and enjoy. In our house, it's better known as Pancake Day. What could be better?

Then . . .

Historically, Shrove Tuesday was the day for Anglo-Christians to confess or 'shrive' their sins and then guzzle a load of pancakes before fasting for Lent, which began the following day, on Ash Wednesday. Pancakes were a good way of using up all the flour, milk and eggs in the house ahead of the fast. Records show that this tradition dated back to the fourteenth century. Both then and now, Shrove Tuesday falls forty-seven days before Easter Sunday, which means it moves around year to year, just like Easter does.

Four hundred years ago, they would give the laziest person in the household the first pancake on Shrove Tuesday. In our house, that would be me, because I love a lay-in! Back then, no one would admit to being the laziest, so the first pancake often went uneaten. Probably for the best, because, in my experience, the first pancake is always the worst, anyway.

At Eton College, the cook used to fasten a pancake to the school's door knocker. I have no idea why. Maybe it was a sign to visitors telling them not to bother knocking, because everybody inside was busy eating pancakes?

In London, the young apprentices of all trades used to play football on the commons on Shrove Tuesday. And, for some reason best known to the king, there was a law that, for this one day only, the apprentices were allowed to break down people's front doors. They mostly chose brothels...

In Scotland and the West Country, at 'Shrovetide', people used to go 'shroving', which essentially meant going around villages and hamlets begging for food, pancakes or money. After a harsh winter, there would be a lot of hunger among the poor. If the request was denied, you could pelt rubbish and old crockery at people's doors, a practice known as 'Lent crocking'. Seems fair enough, to me.

Now...

These days, Pancake Day in the UK is more about food than faith for most of us. It's a similar thing in Iceland, where the day before Shrove Tuesday is 'Bun Day' and you eat buns with jam and cream. Icelandic Shrove Tuesday is called 'Bursting Day' or 'Blast Day', when you eat salted meat and lentil soup until you 'explode'. I'd be asking Marc for a separate bed that night, please!

On Shrove Tuesday in Poland, you eat pastry 'angel wings' dusted in icing sugar for good luck, and doughnuts for more good luck. Yum. In Denmark, it's doughnuts again, and kids swing bats at cat-shaped piñatas filled with sweets. In France it's all about the crepes and waffles, and in Spain, New Orleans and Brazil, they just go wild and have a carnival. Why not?!

When I was growing up, Pancake Day was always a memorable day in our house, because we really went all in and didn't eat much else. I remember coming home from school and seeing a large glass bowl, lots of eggs on the side, piles of lemons and a big bag of sugar.

Now, the age-old debate: what are you having on your pancakes? For me, there's no question – it's got to be lemon and sugar. I will argue 'til I'm blue in the face that it's the best filling for a pancake, but of course, my kids want chocolate spread. That's how customs change and develop, I suppose, because their memories will be of pancakes spread thick with chocolatey, nutty, creamy heaven, whereas mine is of tart, sugary paradise. Maybe in the end, it's not really about the filling, but rather the family time that comes with pancakes being made and served. Those memories are the ones that stick in your mind from childhood days, the times you sat at the kitchen table on a Tuesday after school and someone fried you up something special.

When Dad was living with us, I'd always make him a nice lemon and sugar pancake on Shrove Tuesday. He liked his pancake very well done and crispy. (Weirdly, most people in my family like everything well done, if not burnt to a crisp.)

I think the whole thing is a lovely tradition, even if you're not religious. When I was a child, we never had pancakes apart from on Shrove Tuesday, so they felt even more special. In the same way, we only ever had a hot cross bun at Easter, making it a treat, but Marc is a monster for making pancakes! I would say that at least once a week, Joanie has pancakes. I'm not against it; I just think they deserve to be treated as a special occasion thing. Saying that, though, Marc's brilliant at them – his secret trick is to put a splash of oil in the mixture so that they don't stick to the pan. Don't tell him I told you.

In 2025, it was one of the first times I could remember where I'd been at home for Pancake Day, and as I was making pancakes in the morning and the evening, I knew I'd made the right choice leaving *EastEnders* and having a chance to make more of those special memories with Marc and the kids.

I love the fact that with three simple ingredients – flour, eggs and milk – you can make Yorkshire puddings *and* pancakes. How you balance the ingredients makes all the difference, and I enjoy getting that balance right.

Ingredients are like the tools of life. How things turn out depends on how we use the tools we've been given.

Nat's Perfect Pancake Recipe
2 eggs
100g flour
300ml milk
Splash of oil
Pinch of salt
Makes 6–12

Best Yorkshire Pudding Recipe
2 eggs
140g plain flour
200ml milk
Pinch of salt
Makes 8–24

Chapter Five

Wednesday

So here we are – we've made it to Wednesday! It's 'the hump'; the hill of the week – and it's halfway to the weekend! I always think Wednesday is a day when I feel brighter – good times are coming! Well, unless you work in retail, hospitality or entertainment, in which case maybe today is a day off and the good times are already here . . .

For me, every morning is an open door, regardless of what day it is: I wake up and I step into a world of possibilities, like Mr Benn in the costume shop on that old TV show. Although I may not find myself in a medieval court dressed as a knight like he did, or flying through the air on a magic carpet, I know I'm bound to have my own surprises and challenges as the day unfolds.

I really believe that all you can aim for is to do the best you can in the nicest possible way – and not beat yourself up too much if you fall short. I reckon that was probably Mr Benn's attitude to life, too.

Does it matter how you say Wednesday? Does it signify anything about your background, dialect or preferences?

Northerners often vocalise the 'd', but there are no hard and fast rules – it can be 'Wens-di', 'Wens-day', 'Wednz-di', 'Weddenz-day' or 'Wins-dee'. What's great is that it's one of those words that seems to be said every which way – and no one is bothered. Seems to me that's quite a rare phenomenon these days!

When I think of significant Wednesdays in my life, I think of the Wednesdays I used to go and stay at Wendy Richard's house, back when I was in my twenties. Wendy, who played Pauline Fowler in *EastEnders*, had a gorgeous place in Marylebone in Central London, where she lived in cosy comfort with lovely John, her partner from Northern Ireland, and her beloved Cairn Terrier, Shirley. After a day on set at Elstree filming *EastEnders*, Wendy and I would travel back to her house for a glass of champagne. Very civilized! After that, we'd usually pop to the local curry house for dinner with John and some of their friends, who were just as lovely as they were. Then, once we'd been suitably fed and watered, we'd get into our pyjamas and get comfy before sitting down in Wendy's beautiful lounge to learn our lines together and run through Pauline and Sonia's scenes.

Wendy's character Pauline was my character Sonia's mother-in-law for a while, back when Sonia was married to Pauline's son, Martin Fowler, played by James Alexandrou. Sonia and Martin had a pretty stormy relationship, which meant that Wendy and I were usually yelling at each other as we rehearsed!

She'd shout at me: 'You keep your filthy little lies to yourself, you hear me?'

And I'd scream back: 'You're twisted, and you've always been twisted. Why do you hate me so much?'

Thankfully, Wendy and John's house had thick walls and understanding neighbours! God only knows what they must have thought!

Despite our onscreen spats, Wendy was a dear friend. She was really supportive and someone to lean on after my mum passed, and she instinctively stepped up to give support when I needed it most. Her own father had died in awful circumstances when she was only eleven, so she understood how difficult it was to lose a parent young. She never tried to step in and replace my mum or be a mother figure, though. That wouldn't have worked, partly because her animals were like her children (you wouldn't believe how much she doted on them – no one else could have held a candle up to them!) but also because I was very clear in my mind that Mum was my mum and no one else could come close or take her place. What I really needed was someone warm-hearted and kind by my side – and that was Wendy all over.

One year, just after Mum died, Wendy invited Dad and me for Christmas Day. We went to a pub in Marylebone with John and Shirley, had a bit of dinner and played Scrabble. It was a very, very quiet year, but we couldn't have stayed at home. Our family just wasn't the same without Mum. The whole world felt so much emptier and sadder.

Wendy was a massive TV star throughout her career, but

I'm not sure that many of her younger fans knew that she'd actually made her name as a comic actress before focusing on drama. From 1972 until 1985, she played Cockney sales assistant Miss Brahms in the smash-hit BBC sitcom *Are You Being Served?* alongside the comedy legends that were Mollie Sugden and John Inman – it was regularly watched by more than 20 million viewers. The programme was all innuendo, slapstick and references to Mrs Slocombe's pussy (that is, her cat, Tiddles) and, to be honest, it hasn't aged well. The gender stereotyping and sexism is cringe! If you can overlook all that though, the acting is brilliant, and Wendy's timing and delivery is up there with the best of them.

I don't think Wendy would be at all surprised to see that I'm now taking steps into the comedy world myself, because she saw a knack for comic timing in me early on. In her own autobiography, which came out in 2001, she wrote something like, 'Natalie Cassidy is someone to look out for. I think she could be one of the best comedic actresses of our time.'

It's amazing to think she wrote those words when I was just a teenager! I'm always quite taken aback when I deliver a line and people laugh. It's not intentional, but the actor and comedian Joe Wilkinson has told me that I'm just naturally funny. I take it as a massive compliment, coming from him.

I know Wendy would have been proud to see the work I've done in recent years, especially the comedy cameos and supporting roles in shows like *Psychoville*, *Motherland*, *Mandy* and *Boarders*. Working outside of *EastEnders* has always been on my radar. You'll have seen me on the odd quiz show or Saturday night entertainment show, or on *Comic Relief* and *Children In Need*. Playing other characters has also been important to me – I never just wanted to be Sonia. With the comic roles, the comedy aspect is deep within me because I've grown up watching comedy and I love it so much.

I always feel that I've manifested the roles in some way or another. They haven't just fallen on my lap. I've been vocal about the shows I love. I followed the producers of *Motherland* on Twitter, for instance, and then someone messaged me about doing a cameo. When I did *Motherland*, I spoke to the amazing Diane Morgan and that led to *Mandy*. *Psychoville* really was just sheer luck, but usually, the work has come because I've been proactive.

Wendy starred in the very first episode of *EastEnders* in 1985 and went on to appear in more than two thousand episodes before she left the show in 2006, the year I also decided to leave for the first time. By then, we were the very closest of friends and it was a big blow when she passed in 2009.

Wendy sweetly left me her cigarette holder and her beloved cribbage board. I also have my dad's cribbage board, which he made in woodwork class at school. Wendy and Dad used to talk about cribbage together, but they never actually got around to playing, probably because my dad was a bit rusty by then and I think he was slightly embarrassed about it. 'Oh, I might do,' he'd say. Now I have two cribbage boards – but I don't know how to play! Thinking about it now, since I love Rummy and Whist, perhaps it would be good to remedy that and learn the rules of cribbage. You're never too late to learn something new!

> Have you noticed how often the seasons are used as a metaphor for age? People say, 'She ain't no spring chicken,' and 'He was in the autumn of his life.'
>
> If you applied the same principle to the days of the week, I suppose I'd be in the Wednesday afternoon of my life, maybe tipping towards Wednesday evening. But nobody ever says, 'She was in the midweek of her life,' although I quite like the sound of it. I'm very happy pottering along life on a Wednesday!

I had some other very memorable Wednesdays with Wendy, including the nights we'd go to the National Television Awards (NTAs) with the rest of the *EastEnders* cast – or some of them, at least. Held once a year on a Wednesday, the NTAs is a massive deal for the TV industry; all the faces from the previous year's telly shows come out for a big celebration, and the awards in all the different categories are decided by public vote.

The first few times I went, I found the NTAs was really fun. For me, the best bit of any big night has always been the time before you go: the getting ready, the excitement, who you're going with in the car and who you're going to see when you're there. You get dressed up in your glad rags, and there's a big red carpet to walk along, with cameras flashing and people shouting hello. These days, you'll see the likes of

Claudia Winkleman and Tess Daly from *Strictly*, and you'll see Ricky Gervais, or Ant and Dec from *I'm A Celebrity* . . . Back then, it was people like Brucie, Cilla, Richard and Judy, and Trevor McDonald.

Maybe it's because I'm getting older, but the NTAs felt so much bigger in the Noughties. Do we idealise memories in our heads to give us that sense that things were much better once, when, in reality, things haven't really changed that much? Is this what we do as the years pass? Maybe it's just nostalgia, I don't know, but I always felt very honoured to be at those early NTAs. The whole event had a sense of ceremony about it and it really felt like something special. Everyone was very glamorous, and had clearly pulled out all the stops. The whole thing was very reverential and respectful too; you'd listen to all the awards be read out and applaud the nominees, and you could hear a pin drop in the auditorium when the winners gave their speeches. Contrast that with one of the most recent NTAs I went to, a few years ago, where Sir David Attenborough collected an award, and I couldn't hear him speaking above the noise of people chatting and laughing and getting up from their seats to go to the bar.

I was honestly appalled. 'What's happened?' I thought. 'Where's the level of professionalism you'd expect from the television industry?'

To me, I felt like it came across as self-importance; an attitude that said, 'I can do what I want now, and if I want to get up and talk to somebody then I will, because it's my right to do that.' Call me old-fashioned, but I find things like that to be plain old bad manners.

An awards ceremony is always great for people-watching, and it can a very interesting place, especially if you have your head screwed on and don't get too star-struck! It can also be quite funny – I've definitely had occasions where I'll be chatting to somebody, and they'll be glancing over my shoulder to see if there's anyone better to talk to! The whole thing makes me feel like I'm in an episode of *Extras*. Bizarre!

When I was younger, these big industry nights felt so important that I would often splash out on my outfits or get a dress specially made for me. For the British Soap Awards in 2001, I remember going up near Tower Bridge in London to a wharf of little shops to meet a dressmaker someone had recommended to me. It was just how you'd imagine it: I was measured up in a tiny room crammed with patterns, mannequins and bolts of satin by a seamstress with a tape measure slung over one shoulder and pins and needles sticking out of her lapels.

After leafing through a book of designs, we eventually decided on a corseted evening gown – looking back, it seems ridiculous now because I was eighteen and the style made me look like an old woman! Still, I wore it, and I loved it, and I felt really grown up as I walked down the red carpet in my long, flowy dress that swished around my ankles, with my hair swept up in a sleek chignon bun. I went on to win the Best Actress award that night, which is the sort of moment you dream of as a young actor. Mum and Dad were so proud of me.

Life is never perfect, though, and about halfway through the evening, I started to feel really hot and bothered. I was standing chatting to a group of *EastEnders* cast and crew, and suddenly I felt myself sway; my cheeks were burning, my head was swimming and I felt faint. I hadn't had anything much to drink, and I didn't know what on earth was happening! I tried to take a deep breath to steady myself, but my ribcage couldn't expand properly because my corset was done up so tight, and I started to panic.

Standing next to me was my lovely friend, the director Jamie Annett, and I turned to him in a panic: 'Jamie, you've got to help me undo this thing, because I'm going to fall over any moment!'

The awards were taking place in a massive room that had been done up with black felt wall hangings and fairy lights for sparkle. We found a pocket of darkness in a far corner of the room and Jamie, bless him, started frantically loosening the laces of my corset. It was so tightly done up that he really had to yank at the fastenings – and do it quickly, before I fainted!

Suddenly, an American voice called out, 'Hey, are you okay?'

We peered through the darkness, squinting to see who it was. It turned out to be none other than Jerry Springer, the US talk show host! I hate to think what weird scene he thought he had stumbled upon, what with Jamie tugging at my top in a dark corner, and me bent over telling him to get on with it! No wonder Jerry sounded concerned.

'We're fine, thanks, Jerry!' I panted. 'Absolutely fine.'

Mortifying, but you have to laugh at these things! I never met Jerry again, so I didn't have a chance to explain myself. Hopefully he didn't think too much of it . . .

I used to plan my outfit for weeks before a big awards ceremony, but these days, it's money I don't want to spend anymore, so for the last couple of times I've been happy to do the red carpet in high street clothes. One time, I wore a silver Mango skirt with a white shirt. The year before that, I went in an old green Topshop dress that I found at the back of the wardrobe and thought, 'That'll do.' It was comfortable and I felt good – job done!

The latest award ceremony outfit is from Tesco! I couldn't believe it when I saw it on the rail. It's a gorgeous two piece – a little black printed top and a big black skirt to go with it – and it was only forty-two quid for both. I didn't have to think twice!

I'm not a snob when it comes to brands and things. If I see something I like, I couldn't care less what brand it is, or where it's from. To be honest, it's all about convenience these days. So often, as a mum, you'll run around the supermarket with your trolley getting all the bits you need, food-wise, and then you think, 'I'll just go and quickly look at the clothes . . .' You can grab a jumper or a pair of jeans, and it's great quality, it's affordable, and it washes really well, so I'm all for it.

If I'm not picking up bits with my weekly shop, I buy most of my clothes on the high street – M&S is a favourite, and River Island. I'll go anywhere and buy clothes to be honest.

My one indulgence is that I do like a really nice handbag, even though they are ridiculously expensive. You get knock-offs that look like the real thing, but there's something about going into a posh shop. It's that *Pretty Woman* thing: I don't look a million dollars, but I wander in and it really is nice to say, 'Can I have a little look at that Louis Vuitton bag, please?' Sometimes you get a glass of champagne while you're there too. It's a bit wanky, to be honest, but I have to admit, I love the experience – I'm a total sucker for it. In fact, if I'd saved the money I've spent on bags over the years, I'd probably have enough money to do up my bathroom the way I want it.

I've kept a couple of beautiful, expensive dresses that I've worn to weddings or awards ceremonies over the years, even though I know I'll never fit into them again. But I suppose that's the lovely thing about having girls – you can pass on your handbags and nice statement pieces to them. Sometimes, I'll buy something lovely to wear for an appearance on telly – something like *Loose Women* – and then there will be pictures everywhere of me wearing that outfit, which makes it quite hard to wear it again. So, I'll give it to a friend, or recycle it, or stick it on Vinted and get some pocket money for the girls.

I didn't try on that Tesco co-ord I bought – I never try anything on in a shop. Those changing room lights, getting all hot and bothered – no thank you! I didn't try it on at home, either, I just bunged it in the wardrobe. But I bought a size 12 to be on the safe side, because I tend to vary between a size 10 and a 12, so fingers crossed, it'll be fine! Now, I feel like I'm ready and prepared for the next big event that comes along.

Wait – what about shoes? Well, there's no getting around it: you have to wear uncomfortable shoes to a glitzy awards night. Pumps and trainers are just not flattering on a red carpet. So, I always have to dig out a pair of heels, which might look nice but kill my feet. I suppose you can always slip them off when you're sitting in your seat, but then it's that much harder to jam them back on when you have to get up again. It's just easier to leave them on, despite the uncomfortable sensation that your feet are expanding inside them, like slo-mo Hulk feet.

The fun bit of the evening ends after you've had your drinks in the bar. Just like in that *Extras* episode set at the BAFTAs, the rest is honestly a bit of an anti-climax. Yes, your make-up and hair looks nice – that's good. But you have to just sit in a chair for ages, and there's a lot of being quiet whilst listening to speeches and so on, so you can't even have a good natter with the people at your table. You're not watered, you're not fed. You'll have a couple of glasses of fizz at the beginning, and then you've got a headache by the halfway break because you're dehydrated. By the time you come out of there, you've got a raging thirst and a bit of hanger and you're absolutely starving on the way home, so you end up in a McDonald's drive-thru with a cheeseburger and fries in the lap of your satin gown. Not so glam!

Most of the time, I think I'd be very happy if I never had to go to an awards ceremony again. Saying that, if I'm in a mood where I think, 'Well, I'm not sure who I'm going to see there, and it might be good to chat to a few people,' I can be quite enthusiastic about it and proactive in planning it all. There I go again, contradicting myself. I suppose it just goes to show what a difference your attitude and your mood makes to how we approach life, and how much we enjoy things!

I sometimes need to remind myself that positive things can happen if the stars align while you're out there networking. I went to the TV Choice Awards a couple of years ago and bumped into somebody I hadn't seen for a while. If I hadn't bumped into them, I wouldn't have been offered the chance to do ITV's *The Masked Singer*, which I secretly filmed in the summer of 2024. More on that later. That chance encounter made me realise that it's good to let people know you're around and up for doing things.

The same goes for anyone who is looking for a new job or career change – you've got to get yourself out there and have that conversation, or else, who knows what opportunities you might miss out on? When you're affiliated with a show like *EastEnders* for a long time – and I know I always will be, and it's not a problem – people look at you and think, 'She won't be free for other work.' But when you're out at an event and they ask, 'How's *EastEnders*?' you get the chance to say, 'I'm not there actually. I'm not going to be there now for the foreseeable future.'

It plants seeds in people's heads. And then maybe you can say something like, 'Yeah, I did this thing with Ricky Gervais . . .'

> **The Most Ridiculous Thing Ever #1**
> (My phone rings. The screen shows no caller ID. I'm expect-
> ing a call from the GP, so I pick up.)
> Voice: 'Hello, this is Ricky Gervais.'
> Me, staring wide-eyed at Marc in the kitchen: 'Oh hello, Ricky.'

The downside of these big nights is being pictured in all the papers and magazines, and you're endlessly judged on your outfit and appearance and your weight. There was always a real sense of added pressure when I was younger, and I'd find myself checking to see whether I was in the good or the bad bit of a write-up. These days, I never think of myself as someone who cares what the press says, but when I look back at those early awards ceremonies and the panic I felt about getting it right, I can see that it really did affect me, especially as it was when I was young and in my most formative years.

The tabloid celebrity fashion magazines were particularly basic and brutal back in the Noughties: a photo of you in your outfit would be given a tick or a cross, and I probably got more crosses than ticks for my red-carpet outfits. I was also in *Heat* magazine on a regular basis, getting papped here and there, going to a nightclub or just for a quiet drink, and then the next thing I knew, there'd be an unflattering shot with comments on what I was wearing and how I was looking. Sometimes they weren't very kind.

It was quite common for the paparazzi to goad people by being really rude to them. They wanted them to shout or retaliate so they could get a picture of them looking angry. I think I swore at them once or twice, but not in a manner that meant they could take a picture of me looking horrible. Nevertheless, they still tried taking pictures up my skirt and all that sort of stuff.

I dealt with it. You've got to be thick-skinned to be an actor, and I've always had a very thick skin. If you were well known and chose to go out in the Noughties, you knew that it would probably be a part of the night. You're going out, you're having fun, and you're in the coolest place you can be, so you knew the press were also going to be there. Yes, you could moan about it, and maybe they shouldn't have been there, but they were.

Most of the time, I just shrugged it off when journalists wrote unflattering things about my appearance. I never really spoke to anybody about it; I'd see something in a magazine and dismiss it. What I didn't like was when someone brought a nasty comment or picture to my attention. 'Look, you're in the paper!' they'd say, not realising that you're not really bothered about getting media attention, because they weren't in the public eye themselves.

'What are you showing me that for?' I'd think. 'I wouldn't have seen it if you hadn't pointed it out.'

My worst press attention was yet to come, though, and maybe it's no surprise that it centred around my weight. It's ironic in a way, because I really didn't have an issue with my size growing up, even though I was on television. When I was thirteen, fourteen and fifteen, I went out and ate what

I wanted – McDonald's and whatever else – and I just didn't think about it. I was bigger back then, but I never felt uncomfortable in my body. I think the pressure is different for kids of that age now that they have phones and they're bombarded with all these filtered images of perfect people. Even if they're not seeing it because you're stopping them with parental controls, all their friends are doing it, so they see it anyway.

I don't remember worrying about my size when I was in my late teens and early twenties either. I know I must have been conscious of my weight to an extent, but it really didn't bother me and I never gave much thought to food and dieting. *EastEnders* was a lovely place to work, and no one even hinted that I should lose weight or change my appearance. There was never any bitchiness from anyone; I've been very lucky in not attracting workplace drama, because I know a lot of people have to cope with it, whether it be in an office or an institution.

My Worst Outfits . . .

- I went to Dean Gaffney's birthday party in the early 2000s wearing a pair of baggy cargo trousers, a fishnet top and a big diamanté necklace with letters that spelt out S-E-X. I don't know what I was thinking, but I felt very cool at the time.
- I had a pair of old brown leather boots that I paired with a peach, floral, chintzy knee-length dress, a horrible thing, and an old Lacoste woolly cardigan. I was trying to be quite cool and grungy, but it didn't quite work out.

- A pair of old cargos, a white vest top – and a stars and stripes bandana around my head. Just hideous. My shape was a bit more rotund back then and the tops of my arms were out, which now I tend to hide. But at the time I didn't care.

It was only when I took an extended break from *EastEnders* in 2006 that my body image started to preoccupy me, and there was a good reason for that.

It was my choice to leave the show in 2006. I loved working on *EastEnders*, but it was all I had ever done. I wanted to go out and see the world and try new things. Working on the show meant I missed out on so many of the normal, formative experiences most people go through. Think about it: no girls' holidays, no backpacking, no uni. By 2006, I knew that it was time to see what was out there. Or, at the very least, to book a holiday and read some more books.

Almost as soon as I came out of the show, and before I could get that holiday booked, I was approached by a DVD production team with an offer I couldn't refuse – to make a fitness DVD. Essentially, what I heard was, 'You can get fit and lose loads of weight, and we'll pay you.' It seemed like a win-win situation.

They explained that I'd be working with a trainer and a nutritionist to shape up, slim down and inspire others, and the fee was a hundred grand. Fitness DVDs were big business back then, before we all had Joe Wicks on our phones and endless options for fun and easy ways to work out.

'This is brilliant,' I thought.

Looking back now, older and wiser, the whole thing turned out to be a very bad decision on my part. I lost a huge amount of weight over the next twelve weeks, and it's not normal or healthy to lose so much weight in such a short space of time. Before I knew it, we were doing the 'after' photos and then there was a whirlwind of shoots and press interviews, where I talked about losing seven inches off my waist and was busy encouraging people to 'go for it and watch the old you disappear!'

Natalie Cassidy's Then & Now Workout came out in December 2007, and it was a massive success. It sold a quarter of a million copies, which made me wish I'd asked for a royalty! But there were problems ahead, because as soon as we finished filming, the team went away, and I was left to my own devices. And I just ate and ate and ate.

I quickly put on all the weight I'd lost – way faster than I'd lost it. Soon, I found myself plastered all over the tabloids next to headlines like, 'Natalie, the yo-yo dieter'. Despite my thick skin, it really knocked me for six, and I remember feeling really ashamed of myself. I hadn't cared what other people thought about me before the DVD came out, but I was really young – just 23 – and this weight thing is hard for everyone, particularly when you're in the public eye, and every weight fluctuation is being talked about in magazines and the papers. I tried taking laxatives, eating loads, not eating enough, then trying with the laxatives again . . . it was a vicious circle. Obviously, putting my body through all that contributed to my shaky state of mind, because my body didn't know if it was coming or going, and my brain was experiencing bouts of starvation as well. You wouldn't believe all the hate I had in the media as I struggled my way through it all. There was no compassion and people were really nasty. Looking back, it was an awful time.

When I reflect on the whole experience, I ultimately feel that it had to happen. Why? Well, you learn your lessons, don't you? Okay, it was an extreme way to learn how to develop a new relationship with food, but I think a lot of young women go through a similar process when they're in their twenties, albeit without being the cardboard target in a shooting range, which is what it felt like for a while. Either way, I had to retrain myself in nutrition and eating well, as well as how I felt about my body. Over time, I've really balanced out, and I'm so grateful for that, especially as I've got girls and I want to set them a healthy example, if possible. I know that so many people struggle with eating disorders, or spend their lives jumping from one fad diet to the next, and I feel really lucky that that hasn't been my experience.

I've been roughly the same weight for ages now, although I fluctuate a bit. It's that boring old, common-sense advice, but I find that to keep the weight off, you have to be mindful of what you eat, and eat in moderation, though you still need the odd treat here or there! I fast a little bit as well: I often don't have breakfast; I'll wait for lunch time. I don't consciously think about it, but it just sort of happens with busyness. That won't work for everyone, though. You find your own way that you feel comfortable with. People swear by juicing, keto, fasting and other diets; others maintain their weight by sticking to more traditional foods like stews, curries and meat and two veg. I haven't got a sweet tooth, and I don't sit and eat cake or biscuits, but I do love the savoury – the crisps, the bread – and that's where I fall down because it's all still sugar, but I'm working on it. And life is too short not to enjoy your food!

In my family, we have slow metabolisms. I'm like my brothers – we don't have to eat much to put on weight. It always amazes me when I see people eat breakfast and then tuck into sandwiches and crisps, and then they say they're off to have their dinner. If I ate like they did, I'd be huge.

Tips For Feeling Happier With Your Size

- Try not to get too het up with all the food and diet stuff
- Eat things that are good for you
- Eat what makes you feel better
- Try not to eat loads of it
- Try to be grateful
- Look in the mirror and say, 'I'm so lucky to be here. Let's just celebrate that'
- Let's give ourselves a bit of a break
- And, by the way, when I got to a green 'healthy' BMI, I looked ridiculous, like a lollipop!

In certain situations and locations, I can be somewhere and feel a million dollars and not even think about my weight.

Yet, put me in another situation and location, with another set of people, and I feel like the ugliest person in the room, and I just want to go home. It's because I'm comparing myself to other people. I'm thinking, 'Out of everyone in this room, I'm the biggest person here.' That's not good. There's a great phrase, 'comparison is the thief of joy', and I think there's a lot of truth to that. You know what they say, 'compare and despair', and I know now that there's no point wasting time comparing myself to some underwear model in a magazine, because I just wasn't built to look like that.

Let's try and live: let's eat what we want, when we want, in moderation, and just have fun, and try not to worry about what we look like or compare ourselves to others. If we can all just get up in the morning and think, 'How lucky am I to be here?' and not beat ourselves up about what we look like all the time, or talk about other people and what they look like or compare ourselves, then maybe we'd all be that little bit happier.

With everything that's going on, how can we then beat ourselves up that we haven't been to the gym or been on the Peloton? I got on the Peloton the other day and it was the first time I'd gone on it in a month. I feel so guilty about not using it, when it's just because I've been very, very busy, and that hour I could be exercising, I just want to sit on the sofa, put my feet up and watch the telly. I don't want to feel guilty about that. Guilt brings out bad habits – you think, 'Oh well, I've messed up now,' so you have another packet of crisps, or else you wind up skipping lunch or dinner to make up for it, which is really bad for you. We need to be more like my daughter Eliza.

She'll come in with her chocolate-covered pistachios at nine o'clock at night. I said, 'Liza, are they necessary?'

She says, 'No, they're not necessary, but I really want them, and I don't care about my weight.'

And I think, 'Good for you.' I'm so pleased that, even with all the pressures that teenage girls are facing now, that she has her head screwed on when it comes to things like that. I know it's not easy, but I really hope she can hold on to it as she gets older.

So, try not to beat yourself up, because time is a big factor in this, and all of us are living lives in the here and now – there aren't enough minutes in an hour, enough hours in a day or days in a week. Slowly but surely, we can work out a timetable that means we will have time to do things and time to prepare meals, but sometimes we're not going to have that time. Let's not worry about it too much. It's not a big deal. We're not superhuman and we're all just doing the best we can with what we have. Remember that.

A part of me wishes we could dress like people did in the past. You look back at old photos and films and see the women's neat coiffures, and they're wearing hats and tailored suits and shiny shoes – the fashion was so smart back then. Everybody made the effort: their hair was done, the hats were on and the clothes were pressed; there's just something about it that seems really clean and simple and nice. It's easy to have an idealistic view of a time you weren't living through, but you get the sense that people were more grateful for what they had than they are today, and looked after things more. If you had a hole in one of your garments, you had to darn it, didn't you? You wouldn't throw it away.

When it comes to the clothes you wear, you need to know what suits you and work with that. Which is all very well, until you see something on the hanger and think, 'I love that.' Then you put it on, and it looks like a sack of shit.

I've taken advice from fashion stylists, buyers and wardrobe people. But the people that I rely on for style advice now are my nieces, Maria and Ellia, because they're honest, and I know they want me to look nice. So, I always go to them for an opinion – especially Maria; because she works in fashion. Maria helps me a lot with what I wear – we all need a Maria in our lives! I'd say she's my niece-and-secret-stylist, and I'm very lucky to have her.

I Would Fight Someone Who Tried to Take Away . . .

- My oldest grey nightie. It's from the White Company, long sleeved V-neck, down to the knee. It's the most unglamorous, unsexy piece of clothing, but I just love it, and I can't ever see myself throwing that away.
- My lovely grey woollen maxi coat. I'm obsessed with coats. I could buy a coat every day. I think they really make an outfit.

You Can't Go Wrong With . . .
A nice white shirt and a pair of blue jeans

I take great pleasure in looking lovely and having nice clothes, but there's another part of me that doesn't care what I look like. I will go on Instagram with my hair all over the place and no make-up on, and won't give it a second thought. But I know many, many people who would never, ever put a picture on social media without make-up on.

It takes me five minutes to put on my make-up. Ten minutes max – I'm awful. It all goes on with the hands: foundation goes on; under-eye concealer goes on; then it's blusher, bronzer, lip tint and lip gloss. Finally, I use an eyebrow pencil, because my eyebrows are very important – I'm always raising them! – and a mascara wand.

If I was stranded on a desert island and could only keep one thing, it would be my eyebrow pencil. I plucked my eyebrows to death in the Nineties, as everybody did, and they never grew back, so I need that pencil. I long for bushy eyebrows, like Eliza's, and I'm petrified that she'll be tempted to do what I did. Fortunately, at the moment, bigger brows are in fashion, so she's not touched them.

When it comes to skincare, I have my routine. I never really have facials; I get worried about face treatments because I've got good skin, and I don't want to mess around with it. It's not about what I drink, or what I put on it. It's genetic. My mum had nice skin and so did my Nanny Liz.

Although I don't pamper myself very much, this year I took two of my friends to Champneys for a night and we had a massage and enjoyed the spa and ate nice healthy dinners. It was blissful – not just not having to squeeze in an hour's walk and a coffee in between school runs and work and cleaning and routine, but having a whole thirty-six hours together to really enjoy each other's company and be pampered a bit.

I've never had any Botox, never done anything to my face, except for the chemical peel I had about a year ago. I had it done at home, and it stung quite a lot. Afterwards, my skin didn't feel like my skin anymore. Not to be repeated.

There's a lot of pressure on women to stay looking young, and I think that pressure can be even worse when you're in the public eye and your picture is appearing all over the place. On Instagram and social media, with all the filters and whatnot, it's easy to compare yourself to other people. I'd never say never to having Botox though. I've got a couple of little lines that have started to appear around my mouth that I don't like, but I love my crow's feet, and at the end of the day, they're all laughter lines, aren't they? Funnily enough, I think I've had an instant facelift since leaving *EastEnders*, because I'm not frowning and shouting every day, creating those ingrained forehead lines. I'm not constantly upset or crying as part of a scene, and that's quite liberating in itself, not doing the misery.

There's so many new fads that come and go, and it can

seem like everyone's being injected with this or that, which is fine if that's what you want, but at the end of the day, I think skin is like health, or anything else. If it ain't broke, don't fix it.

Chapter Six

Thursday

If Thursday were a person, I feel that it would be very chic. Whatever the fashion was, you'd always want to look like Thursday – feather boa, cigarette holder and all.

Maybe I feel that way because Thursday evening used to be *the* night to go out in London when I was a teenager. In the late Nineties and early Noughties, it was the cool night out at the cool clubs with the cool people. I was very young when I started going out clubbing – I was only fourteen, maybe fifteen, and back then things were very different. Door policy is obviously much stricter now, but if you were on the telly in the late Nineties, you could get in anywhere, as long as you were old enough to smudge some kohl around your eyes – I'd often be out and about in Sugar Reef or the Velvet Rooms with friends and work colleagues.

"Hello Sonia, in we go!" said the friendly bouncers.

We went to a different club every night. Inside, there would be a table stacked with drinks just for us. Absolute shambles! We used to drink champagne, or vodka and Red Bull, and stay up late, although I couldn't drink alcohol if Patsy Palmer was out with us. She wouldn't let me near it until I was older;

she was very strict about that, just like a real-life big sister. But I made up for it when she wasn't around.

Things are different now and I would be petrified if Eliza was going out and about like I used to. Fortunately, I think her generation are much more health-conscious and would rather be at the gym or checking out some cool new milkshake shop because it's Instagrammable. They love their clothes and their shopping. We did as well, but they seem more style-aware and into their make-up. They're not afraid to be who they want to be, but I just think they're great. They get a lot of stick, but I think they're an improvement on us, to be honest!

In the late Nineties, *Top of the Pops* was filmed in a studio in Borehamwood, where *EastEnders* is filmed, and we all shared a canteen and a bar. It was brilliant, because you'd run over to the bar and canteen to see who was in that night. You'd get the inside information from the *Top of the Pops* crew and go into a rehearsal and watch Take That perform 'Never Forget', and meet them afterwards. I met Ocean Colour Scene and watched Toploader perform 'Dancing in The Moonlight'. I'll never forget knocking on the door of the Spice Girls' dressing room door and getting a Polaroid picture with them. They were huge! I once met Liam Gallagher and the rest of Oasis in a bar, and Liam shouted, 'Oi Sonia, where's your trumpet?' I'd loved Oasis since I was a teenager, and it was amazing to think that all the pop stars knew who we were.

In later years, I'd go to a club in Soho called Pop, with Ian Watkins – H from Steps – and the actor Adam Garcia. If I was working the next day, often I wouldn't have a drink so that

I could drive into London, have a night out and drive home. But one particular evening, H and I went out and ended up on the front of the *Sun* newspaper the next morning. The headline was, 'H and Nat step out,' or something like that.

As I walked past the costume room on my way into work the next morning, I saw Barbara Windsor in there. Barbara loved looking at the papers. She happened to have the *Sun* in her hand, and she held it up. 'I hope you're not late today, and I hope you're not too tired,' she said with a smile.

It wasn't a telling off; it felt more like a gentle warning, to say, 'Remember, you're working. Be careful. It's fine to be stepping out of clubs, but don't start falling out of them, young lady.' I definitely took it on board.

H and I still text each other every now and again. He's a lovely, lovely guy. These days, we're not heading out for a night out together – more often than not, it's one of us asking the other for a favour, to give something, or do something for a charity. And then we'll remind each other of something silly that happened during our clubbing days.

When I was in my teens and twenties, I always wanted to be out. In my twenties, I used to love going to the 100 Club on Oxford Street, where they had indie music nights and we jumped around to The Smiths and Pulp with a can of Red Stripe.

Five Club Anthems That Remind Me of That Time

- 'Free' – Ultra Naté
- 'Ready For The Floor' – Hot Chip

- 'A Little Bit of Luck' – DJ Luck & MC Neat
- 'Teardrops' – Lovestation
- 'Sincere' – MJ Cole

Top 5 Indie Songs
- 'Whatever' – Oasis
- 'Parklife' – Blur
- 'Common People' – Pulp
- 'Alright' – Supergrass
- 'There Goes the Fear' – Doves

I did quite a few things I probably shouldn't have done when I was younger: I bunked off school a couple of times; I went to nightclubs when I was underage and drank cocktails before I was legally allowed to.

I think I've turned out all right, so I suppose I could say, 'Well, it didn't do me any harm.'

That's what people always say, isn't it? 'It didn't do me any harm.' But just because you turned out fine, how do you know that having the same experiences won't harm someone else?

Maybe bunking off school wasn't great for me, or going to nightclubs so young, either. I don't know, but we're back to that 'knife edge' my brother Tony talks about. Things could have gone very wrong for me. You see it happen to a lot of people who are famous from a young age. Luckily, I was always very grounded.

My daughter Eliza isn't in the same position as I was, but I wouldn't let her do the things I did because I am her mum and I'm here to guide her through her childhood. When I was fourteen and fifteen, my mum was so protective of me that I wouldn't tell her when I wanted to go out or be honest about where I was going. Instead, I'd say I was going to my mate's house and then my friend's mum would feel sorry for me and say, 'Go on. You can go out. Your mum won't know.' I'm sure, like most teenagers, Eliza gets up to some stuff I don't know about. If she does, hopefully it's not harmful to her. But I can't just say, 'Fine, bunk off and go down the canal with a can of cider; it didn't do me any harm . . .' I have to parent her in today's world and do what's right for her.

It's funny: as your children grow up, you realise more and more what your own mother lived through when you were a teenager. *Was I really like this at fourteen?* I think, when I've just been dished a load of teen attitude. *Did my poor mum have to put up with this?* (Yes, she did.)

As much as it's lovely and we do have great times, the teen years are hard years to navigate. With Eliza, if there's a problem at school, or a fallout with a friend, she'll say 'You're not fifteen, Mum – you don't understand!'

I'm sure I said the same to my mum many times – and now I'm on the receiving end. Oh, the irony of life! 'Give me a break, Eliza,' I tell her. 'I've never had a fifteen-year-old girl before; I'm doing this for the first time, as well.'

When I was fifteen, my mum, dad and I moved out of London to Broxbourne in Hertfordshire, not so far from where I live now. They were after a more peaceful, greener life and wanted to be nearer my brother David and his family.

I liked it there, too, and it was only eighteen miles from Elstree. When I went out clubbing, I'd just get cabs there and back. When I was a few years older, if I was out really late and had to be on set early the next morning, I'd get a cab straight to work and sleep in my dressing room. I'd get there by about four-ish, put my head down for a few hours and go into make-up at half seven! The security guards at work were my best friends. 'That's all right, Nat. Don't tell anyone.'

My mum didn't like me going out god-knows-where – and there were no tracker apps on your smartphones then. But at that age, I always wanted to be out with friends. Like a lot of teens, I was selfish; I didn't think of my mum and how she might be feeling after the upheaval of moving away from the area she'd grown up in and raised a family. In fact, Mum didn't like change and I don't think she coped very well when they left London. She felt anxious not having the routines that had kept her grounded, like going up to Chapel Market and M&S, and friends and neighbours popping in. It can't have helped that I was off all the time and difficult to pin down. Now, as an adult, I regret not spending more time at home.

Sometimes you follow a crowd that you shouldn't and during that period, I had a group of friends who weren't very nice, though I didn't see it that way then. They were possessive; they wanted me all to themselves and tried to control who else I saw. I didn't like being alone, so I probably wasn't as picky about my friends as I should have been. It must have been difficult for Mum to see me going in the wrong direction, but I wasn't listening to her advice about whether this person or that person was a good influence on me – like every young person, I thought I knew best.

Age-Old Phrases of Mum and Dad
- 'You wait till your dad gets in . . .'
- 'What did your last slave die of?'
- 'It's in one ear, out the other . . .'
- 'I'll give you something to cry about . . .'
- 'Who do you think you are, the Queen of Sheba?'
- 'Here she is, Lady Muck!'
- 'Were you born in a barn?'

Are people better parents before they've had kids, as the saying goes? I'm sure I was. I never thought I'd shout at my kids, but I can be very impatient, and I'm a bit of a shouter at times. It doesn't happen often, and I feel guilty about it when it does, but I'm also aware that my attitude is slightly old-fashioned. There's a part of me that thinks you have to respect your elders, and I can get quite fired up about it.

The idea that everyone is equal and we've all got to listen to each other is fine, up to a point. But if you've birthed someone and you're trying to bring them up in the right manner, I feel you should have more power than they do. Kids need boundaries and, as a parent, you're the one that needs to be setting those boundaries. They need to know where they stand.

Mind you, we are a new generation of parents, so although it's tempting to say, 'How dare you speak to me like that?', just like my mum said to me, it's probably more powerful to let them know the effect their words are having on you. Instead of putting up your proverbial fists and raising the temperature, you can often diffuse an argument with a teenager by saying, 'It really hurts me when you speak to me like that, you know.'

*

Even though I'm not out clubbing much these days, I feel like Thursday is an acceptable night to have a drink. You've done the hump – you've got through Wednesday – and you can relax a bit as the weekend approaches, which is why some people call it 'Thirsty Thursday' or 'Friday's Friday'. I think for me it stems from the idea that Thursday night is *the* night to go out. A Thursday drink has stuck with me, so even when I'm in at home, that's my night out.

Friday, I can take it or leave it – I'm not fussed about drinking on a Friday. Even on a Saturday, I'm not really bothered – given a choice, I'd probably rather just jump straight into Sunday, which is the other day for alcohol in my week, because it can be a long day of cooking a lovely roast dinner for everyone and enjoying a nice glass of wine or two.

In my mind, Monday is not an evening for drinking. Don't get me wrong, the odd tipple on a Monday, Tuesday or a Wednesday is always welcome – and you might make an exception if there's a new baby in the family, or a funeral, or a Christmas work party on a Monday in December . . . or any other reason, really!

I do enjoy a drink. Once you get a bit older, you've got to be a bit more careful with it, because if you drink too much, it's not just a hangover anymore, is it? It's a couple of days of feeling rubbish. I don't like feeling that way, but I still do it every now and again, and then I hate myself for it! Some things you never learn!

Even though I do love a bit of booze in the right setting, I know I'm not an alcoholic because if someone opens a bottle of bitter plonk, I'd rather drink water. Saying that, drinking is habitual, so you always have to keep an eye out. It can be dangerous if you get into drinking at home – and we do. A glass of wine quickly turns into a bottle when there's two of you, chatting away. I don't beat myself up for it, but I try to be mindful to make sure I'm not overdoing it.

Can you tell a person by what they order at the pub? There is a corner of the internet crammed with articles by people (mainly ex-bartenders) who think you can. They say things like, 'Wine drinkers are social butterflies', 'Rum-lovers tend to be sensible', 'Beer-swillers are boring' and 'If you like a Bloody Mary, you're a thrill-seeker!'

I think to myself, 'Who on earth reads these articles?!'

My mum wasn't a drinker at all. She loved her tea. But at Christmas, she'd either have a Baileys or a snowball, which is a cocktail made with lime juice, lemonade and advocaat (egg yolks, brandy, vanilla and sugar) with a maraschino cherry for garnish. My dad always enjoyed a whisky – a Bell's or a Famous Grouse. He wasn't a pub-goer; he preferred having a drink at home in front of the telly with Mum.

I enjoy a cold glass of rosé in the garden on a summer's evening and I might have a lager or a stout in a country pub after a windswept walk on holiday in Ireland or Cornwall. But my thing is gin, really. I love everything about gin, from the bottles, to the way it's made – the ingredients and all the different varieties that have sprung up over the last ten years or so. I love it so much that last Christmas, Marc bought me a year-long membership to a craft gin club that sends me a bottle of gin and a magazine every month. Brilliant gift!

According to the internet, gin drinkers can be anything from sophisticated and cool to psychotic. I wonder, does it make a difference that I'm not a fan of flavoured gins? I like my gin plain and dry, and I drink it with Fever Tree tonic water and a slice of lime, which hopefully edges me away from the psychopath end of the gin drinkers' spectrum.

Three Good Reasons to Have a Gin and Tonic
1. The juniper berries in gin have antioxidant, anti-bacterial and anti-inflammatory properties.
2. Gin contains remedial plant extracts, known as botanicals, like coriander seeds, angelica root, bog myrtle(!), rosemary, black pepper and cinnamon.
3. Tonic water was invented in Islington (yes, really!) and it contains quinine, which helps to bring down a fever and can keep mosquitoes at bay when you're on holiday.

Put all of these health benefits together, I'm amazed that gin doesn't work as its own hangover cure. Wouldn't that be great?

Nat's Gin Awards

1. In first place, and currently my favourite brand, is **Monkey 47**, which is made with 47 botanicals from the Black Forest in Germany.
2. A close second is **Cambridge Dry**, filled with individually distilled botanicals that capture the essence of all four seasons.
3. Third place goes to **St Ives Gin**, which is bursting with fragrant botanicals foraged from along the Cornish coast.

Best of the Cocktails and Mocktails

- Negroni
- Equal parts gin, vermouth and Campari, on the rocks
- Kir Royale
- 1/10 creme de cassis (blackcurrant liqueur) and 9/10 champagne
- Mojito
- Rum, soda water, lime juice, sugar, mint leaves
- Sparkling Sunrise
- Equal parts nosecco (or sparkling grape juice or ginger ale) and orange juice. Splash of grenadine
- Summer crush
- Watermelon, strawberries, lime, and ice, blitzed
- Nojito

- Pineapple juice, soda water, mint leaves, lime and a spoonful of sugar, shaken up in a cocktail shaker and strained

What makes Thursday chic? Chic is one of those things that is hard to pin down, but you know it when you see it. There's a hint of rebellious, don't-care confidence in being chic – and, for me, Thursday has that, too.

The word 'chic' entered the English language around 1860 and was pronounced 'chick'. As in, 'So *chick*, darling!' Linguists argue about its origins: does it come from the French word, 'chicanerie', which once meant 'legal quibbling or trickery', or from the German word, 'schick', meaning 'skill' or 'tact'? The German option sounds more likely, and yet you think of 'chic' as being a French trait, don't you? It's, *'Le freak, c'est chic!'* not *'Le freak, das ist schick.'*

Nowadays, 'chic' gets bolted onto any old style idea: hippie, boho, shabby, heroin, geek and checkout chic included. But when I talk about Thursday being chic, I like to think I'm using it in the pure sense, the way it was used to describe cool, young Parisians – *chicards* – from the mid-nineteenth century onwards. It meant more than being fashionable: if you were chic, you were stylish, original and edgy. Fast forward a century, and you see it in French New Wave movies of the 1950s, with cool girls wearing berets and their boyfriends' clothes, throwing caution to the wind and taking two lovers at the same time. Chic is very, very Paris. But to me, it's also a Thursday night out in a London club when you're a teenager.

Going to a nightclub is so exciting when you're first doing it. You're clueless and pretending you're not; you're watching the people in front of you to see how they're doing everything. 'Be cool!' blasts the voice in your head.

You get past the queue and arrive at the foyer and front of house to blag the list or pay the entry fee. The door separating you from the club is tantalisingly *just there*, a few dizzying steps away, the gateway to another portal. When you go through it for the first time – and quite a few times after that – it blows your mind with its intergalactic weirdness. It's like going from black and white into colour, from silence to mega-noise, from mediocrity to opulence. And in the London clubs of the late Nineties and Noughties, there were all these out-there characters walking around as if they owned the place. I absolutely loved it.

It felt like the world was changing and loosening up. There was a feeling of freedom, especially for young women. You had the Spice Girls spreading their message of self-belief and self-empowerment, you had the media ladettes smashing it at work by day and drinking the guys under the table by night, and you had a new intake of women MPs shaking things up in Parliament. It felt like you could do anything a man could: you could ace your job, get pissed on pints and shout your mouth off in public, while stomping around in a pair of jeans and a T-shirt (or a mini dress and boots – totally your choice, babe). You could do all of this and be working class and have a regional accent as well. Superb.

I had a regular crowd of friends I went clubbing with on a Thursday. It was all about having a laugh and messing around in the VIP section of whichever club we were in, and it was probably quite annoying for the other 'VIPs' to have me in their space, if I'm honest. I remember seeing Róisín Murphy, the singer from Moloko, in a club one night and thinking it would be hilarious to sing her song 'back' to her. I don't think she liked me very much for that, I can't lie! I can't blame her for it, either – it wasn't her fault she didn't have a flipping sense of humour that night! There I go channelling my clubby teen self again . . . Maybe those days aren't as far behind me as I think . . .

For a few years, one of the best club nights in Central London was Twice as Nice, DJ Spoony's garage and R&B night at The End in Holborn. I'll never forget having a chat with Victoria and David Beckham at a Twice as Nice do in 2000, not long after they'd got married. It was a huge night for me – we went there after a *Smash Hits* party where I had won the Best TV Actress award. I was only seventeen and in total shock and wonder at this achievement. There's a picture from that night of me and Jack Ryder, who was playing my onscreen boyfriend, Jamie Mitchell, at the time, and it still does the rounds now on all the Huns socials, where they take the piss and compare us to Kate Winslet and Leonardo di Caprio in *Titanic*. There's such a sweetness to it because Jack and I were amazingly close, just like brother and sister. My mum loved him, and he used to stay over all the time. We would have done anything for each other. We were really tight.

I was getting a lot of attention because I was tackling some really big storylines as Sonia on *EastEnders*. In 2000, Sonia gets pregnant after having sex with Martin Fowler and doesn't realise she's expecting until she starts giving birth in the lounge at home, poor thing. Having a hidden pregnancy is actually more common than you'd think, even off the telly, but it's obviously a terrifying experience for a fifteen-year-old to go into labour without warning. It tested my acting abilities to have to register pain, shock and fear all at once, as Big Mo from next door abruptly tells Sonia that she's not dying, she's having a baby!

It was a gift for me because I was only young, and suddenly I was at the top of the show. Having a big storyline like that can be make or break for an actor, and I knew it. When you're given an opportunity, you've got to grab it with both hands and do the best you can, so I did my research, and I went for it. Thankfully, it went down well. It's a scene a lot of people remember from the show, all these years later. And then I went and 'gave birth' on screen again for the *EastEnders* fortieth anniversary live episode! Terrifying.

While all of this was happening, Mum went to the doctor with stomach problems and was diagnosed with bowel cancer, which was such a terrible shock for us all. The whole experience was awful, as she then had go through radiotherapy, an operation, and a stoma procedure, and she hated all of it. It feels horrible to say, but I wasn't around for her as much as I should have been while she was going through all of that. I was so selfish when I was seventeen.

Some of my family say I'm exaggerating to myself about how bad I was, but I don't think I am. The kindest explanation would be that I was living through that time in a state of denial, distracting myself from what was happening to Mum with work and friends.

I simply wasn't able to contemplate a world without Mum – your mum's your mum; she's a fact, a fixture of your life, and you really don't expect her to go anywhere.

I was relieved, but not that surprised, when Mum responded to treatment and the cancer went away. I don't know whether or not Mum, Dad and my brothers tried to shield me from the worst of it. Maybe I wasn't aware of how serious it had been. When Mum cheerfully told me she was cancer-free, I just thought, 'Great, she's better and that's an end to it.'

Thursday Thoughts

Thursday is Thor's-day. He's the one you probably remember from school because his name is easy to remember, and he was the most exciting deity, the Norse god of thunder, lightning and storms. Thor is the Anglo-Saxon version of the Roman god Jupiter.

In Russia, China and the Balkans, Thursday gets its name from being the fourth day of the week. In Greek, Portuguese, Arabic, Hebrew, Vietnamese and Malaysian, it's the fifth day. But there's an episode of *Friends* where Joey controversially claims it is the third day. So, who is right?

It's one of the funniest ever lines from *Friends*, which I loved when I was growing up. Joey explains to Chandler that he thinks of Monday as 'one-day', while Tuesday is 'two-day'. He dismisses Wednesday with a 'when? Huh? What day?', making Thursday the third day. 'Okay?'

Important things happen on a Thursday: UK elections; Australian movie premieres; Thanksgiving; late-night shopping – and since I started this whole book-writing business, I've learned that books always come out in the UK on a Thursday too, although in America they come out on a Tuesday. Who knew?

Pea soup is traditionally eaten in Finland and Sweden on a Thursday, and it's considered a good day for fasting among religious people of many different persuasions – especially the ones who don't like pea soup!

Ultimately, Thursday is a day like any other, just like all the other days, and its meaning depends on where you live, how you think and what you believe.

Another reason that Thursday is dear to my heart is because it was on Thursday, 2 December 1993 that Sonia Jackson first appeared on the telly. It was also always the day when everyone at *EastEnders* got their new production schedule for the following week.

While the daily schedule gives you the director's shot list and tells you where and when everyone will be needed on the day, the Thursday call sheet details which days you will and won't be working during the week to come. Each week,

I was always desperate to find out when I'd be needed on set, so that I could plan the rest of the week around my kids and school, my partner, dentist, doctor, friends and everything else. You could only ever know what was happening a week in advance, which meant no booking seats at the theatre in advance, or tickets to a concert, because you never knew if you'd actually be free to go.

Working on *EastEnders* is absolutely a privilege, and I wouldn't change my time there for the world, but there is a sense of it being relentless because there's no end to it. It's not a drama series in twelve parts, or a play that must close by a certain date; it runs and runs, and so you can never say to yourself, 'When this is over, I'll get the car sorted/rearrange the spice rack/look into holiday activities for the girls.' You have to squeeze everything in here and there when the schedule allows. On the plus side, it does mean that you can suddenly find yourself with two weeks off, if your character isn't needed on set. But when you're filming back-to-back, you're immediately speed-dialling your GP or finding out about car insurance the moment you get a break.

Part of what I think makes *EastEnders* so popular is that it reflects real life. Fans and viewers get to see the characters in close-up as they develop and go through all their ups and downs – in my case, people literally saw me growing up on-screen, from that little ten-year-old blowing a trumpet to a fifteen-year-old in labour. Sonia went on to give baby Chloe up for adoption (she was renamed Rebecca/Bex), got engaged twice to her boyfriend Jamie Mitchell, lost him after he was fatally injured in a car accident, abducted Chloe from her guardian, had a lesbian affair, and was wrongly convicted of the murder of Pauline Fowler – all that before I reached twenty-two and decided it was time for a break from the show after twelve years!

The Christmas Day episode in 2002, where Sonia sits by Jamie Mitchell's bedside in hospital, knowing he will not survive being run over by Martin Fowler, and Jamie slowly realises that he's dying, was a shocker for the sixteen million viewers who sat down to watch it. It was a real challenge for me to do those scenes, because, through Sonia, I was channelling emotions that I'd been experiencing myself for real only a few months earlier, when I lost my mum.

Mum's passing happened a week after my birthday, on 20 May 2002. We went round to lunch with her and Dad on the Sunday. We were all there; Mum made the lunch, and she was fine. It was a really nice day. But on the Monday morning, we had a phone call to say that she'd had an aneurysm. She'd come out the shower and collapsed into Dad's arms.

It's so strange to think that she'd come all through her cancer treatment and out the other side, only to leave us out of the blue like that. It really does make you think, 'Does everybody have their time?'

It was a devastating shock to lose Mum without warning like that, and the days and weeks that followed passed in a blur. I was only nineteen, and looking back, I can see how very young that was to lose a parent. But I internalised my feelings quite quickly. Soon, I was out and about again;

I threw myself into work and being with friends, albeit the wrong group of friends. By then, I had bought my own flat just down the road from Mum and Dad, so I wasn't living at home. Real friends, with my best interests at heart, would have said, 'You need to go round to your dad's and be with your family.' But these friends wanted to isolate me and have me to themselves.

Even if you could excuse my friends for being too young to understand, they had parents who should have known better. I know what I would do if Eliza had a bereaved friend who was always round at ours: I would take the daughter home and say, 'You can call on us anytime, but you need to be at home with your family.'

I think it would have made a huge difference to what happened next if I'd had a more supportive group of people around me. It was my fault for being swayed, but my friends had a hold on me and wouldn't let go. It played a major part in how I handled the situation, and I feel angry about it, all these years later.

I'm in a far stronger place now, but looking back, I can say that I wasn't really all right from the age of nineteen, when my mum passed, up until I was about thirty, after I'd come out of my turbulent relationship with Eliza's birth father and gone back to *EastEnders*. I may have seemed okay on the outside, and honestly, if you'd asked me, I'd have told you that I was fine, but I made some awful decisions and did some stupid things, probably out of grief. No one escapes it: when a parent dies, you have a hole in your life, and you try and fill it however you can. I think I stayed with the wrong friends because I was lonely. Unsurprisingly, I was not in a good place after I'd lost my mum; I was a bit of a mess and probably should have gone for some help.

My brothers Tony and David got on with looking after Dad. Then, within four months, Dad made a snap decision to move to Lincolnshire to be near his brother in the countryside. It was the right move for him because all his life he had wanted to go back to where he'd been evacuated during the war, but it left me on my own, aged nineteen. Even though I still had family around me, my parents had gone, and I was at a very impressionable age.

People ask me if it was weird doing those scenes between Sonia and Jamie, and the scenes of grief that Sonia acted out in the episodes that followed. It did feel strange, but I just had to get on with it. There is a form of psychotherapy that uses theatre techniques to explore personal problems and there I was, doing it without even knowing it, and without really talking to anyone about the feelings that it brought up. I had more scenes like this when Sonia's mum Carol was diagnosed with breast cancer in 2014. That was tough. Even though I was playing my emotions through Sonia, it felt very raw, and those tears on-screen were very real tears that I cried.

Eventually, I realised that my friends weren't good for me, and I left them behind. I also got over Dad upping and leaving for Lincolnshire; I'd always been a daddy's girl at heart, and we started to bond again. Dad had never been abroad before, so I got him a passport and took him to Rome for a couple of weeks, just me and him, which was brilliant. Another time, we went to La Manga, where he played golf, and I did his caddying. We had some great times together and became so, so close; I only wonder how close I would have been with Mum if she'd been around, because Dad and I were like glue.

When it comes to my friends, I've never been afraid to cut people out. Is that really harsh? Some people might think so, but I see it as a positive thing. If people aren't giving you what you need in life, you shouldn't have them around.

There are two types of people: the radiators and the drainers. And I think that if you want to be content, you should stick with the radiators. You haven't got to agree with me, but I guarantee it will help if you're looking to be content. Happiness is linked to not being false, and I just can't be false. Be who you want to be. Don't be scared to just *be*.

Sonia's dramatic storylines continued and reached a climax in 2006, when she was arrested for Pauline's murder and driven off in a police car. Her neighbours watched her go – people she'd known since she was a little kid of ten – shaking their heads and murmuring that she's guilty, although (spoiler!) it would eventually turn out that the real killer was Pauline's husband Joe.

When Sonia was cleared and released from custody, she decided to emigrate to America – and just like that, I left

EastEnders behind me. It was an amicable departure, and the producers wished me all the luck in the world. But after it was announced that I was going in April 2006, a fellow actor, who I shan't name – not a regular – said to me, 'Why are you leaving? It's not like you're going to go and do Chekhov.'

I decided to take this offhand remark as a challenge rather than an insult. After twelve years at *EastEnders*, I felt I'd earned my stripes as an actress and was looking to branch out and explore new things, so why not Chekhov? 'You know what?' I thought. 'Eff you! That's exactly what I'm going to do: a Chekhov play!'

My last scenes in *EastEnders* were filmed in December 2006, and about a month before that, I auditioned for two stage roles that were coming up in 2007: a three-week tour in *The Vagina Monologues*, which I hoped would give me a feel for the theatre again, followed by a country-wide tour of the Alan Ayckbourn comedy, *Bedroom Farce*.

I hadn't been on stage since I left Anna Scher's and I couldn't help remembering how nervous I'd been in her classes. Although I had a lot more acting experience from working on a soap back-to-back, with TV you have the opportunity to muck it up and then do it again – there's the chance for another take. On stage, performing live, it isn't a dress rehearsal – you can't mess up your lines and ask to try again. It's the real thing every night.

To my delight, I was offered both shows, and was lucky enough to share the bill with some great people: Rhona Cameron and Sue Holderness in *The Vagina Monologues*, and

Ben Porter, Tim Watson, Beth Cordingly, Hannah Yelland, Colin Baker and Louise Jameson in *Bedroom Farce*. Both were an absolutely brilliant experience, and I especially loved the challenge of *Bedroom Farce*. It was such a contrast to *EastEnders*. Ayckbourn writes very precisely and you can't paraphrase the text or fudge it if you forget a line – you need to know it one hundred per cent, spot on, in order to get the comic timings. It was a sharp learning curve, especially as I wanted Kate, my character, to be sweet, polite, funny and entirely different from Sonia. She was the first comedic role I played.

Bedroom Farce was a number one tour, booked into all the best venues available. It lasted for three months, and I felt very grown up, driving my little car off to Llandudno in North Wales with my music blaring, and then on to Bath, and then the next place. We played each theatre for a whole week and stayed in digs. Of course, I wanted to move to every town we played in.

We had good audiences on the whole, although I do remember hearing snoring during the odd matinee. That always made me giggle. And it was hard to keep it together when Colin Baker made one particular speech in the play about pilchards. You know when a thing becomes a thing, it becomes another thing, doesn't it? And that's what happened with Colin's pilchards speech, unfortunately, because Colin was such a funny man, both on and offstage.

Just under a year later, I started rehearsals for *The Cherry Orchard*, a play by none other than the Russian playwright (drum roll, please . . .) Anton Chekhov! I played Dunyasha, a housemaid caught up in a love triangle, and I was acting alongside Dame Diana Rigg, Jemma Redgrave, Maureen Lipman and Frank Finlay – all total legends of the theatre. I had an amazing time, but it was also nerve-racking because every single night at the very start of the play, I was first out on the stage, on my own, in the dark, and I had to light a candle. It was the worst! Once I'd done it, I'd be all right, but it was always daunting. 'Will I be able to light it first time? What if I mess it up?' I can't imagine doing that now. Believe it or not, all these years later, I'm still petrified of the stage and of live TV performances. My lips go dry, I start to shake – it's honestly awful!

The Cherry Orchard opened the Chichester Festival in May 2008. The weather was gorgeous, and Chichester was an idyllic place to spend the summer; we used to go off to the beach and explore the Witterings and other Sussex beauty spots. It was very actor-y, which I loved, especially the times when I'd get to go to the pub with Frank Finlay and sit and listen to his wonderful stories: 'When I was working with Laurence Olivier . . .' and 'Back when I was at The National . . .' Diana Rigg was lovely, as well. We discovered a magical drink in a pub in the depths of Sussex, a champagne cider, made with apples using the 'champagne method'. It seemed like the perfect shabby-chic drink for two actors playing Chekhov, especially on a warm summer's day.

I'd love to challenge myself and do theatre again, to see if I can still do it. I think it's probably quite important for me to try to at some stage – although maybe something very small, in case I completely fail. But I would like to try because I don't know whether it's just something that's crept up on me and I now have severe stage-fright. It's important to do things that scare you sometimes!

When you wake up in the morning, anything can happen. A phone call, a knock at the door, a sudden realisation: life can change in a second, for better or for worse. And with 86,400 seconds in a day, the possibilities are endless . . .

Scientific breakthroughs are one-a-penny in this brave new world of AI and massive telescopes. Astrophysicists can see further into space than ever before and say that they have proof that we live in a multiverse. But, even without factoring in the possibility that our universe is constantly splitting into alternate versions, where an infinite number of copies of you and me are living multiple lives in different dimensions, a day as we know it is rarely 'just' a day, is it? Because however humdrum and predictable it appears when you press the snooze button for the seventh time at the crack of dawn, the reality is that it could go a multitude of different ways.

Everything that happens has a knock-on effect; a butterfly effect, if you will. Every delay has a consequence: a late train, a flat tyre, a queue, indigestion, a hole in the roof, a burst of sunshine, a chance encounter, an accident . . .

And life is full of surprises. Maybe you'll find a diamond ring in a puddle, like a friend of mine once did, or discover that your husband has another wife and family living hundreds of miles away. (I've only ever read about this, but the idea fascinates me. How? Why?) Or maybe nothing much will happen, apart from the milk unexpectedly going off, and at the end of the day, you'll put on your pyjamas and head to bed with a shrug. And on those days, we should remember how lucky we are. Plus, some days, getting into bed can be the best part of the day.

*

My departure from *EastEnders* had been announced as a 'break' by the producers, but I felt I'd closed the door and wasn't going back, or not for the foreseeable future. Then Patsy, who played Sonia's sister Bianca, went back in 2008 and soon, she was calling for my return. Patsy often said in interviews that she thought of me and the rest of the Jacksons as family, and in a funny way we really were. But I wasn't ready to go back – I was busy enjoying spreading my wings. Still, I've long learned you can't say no to Patsy, and I was happy to do a couple of guest stints, and of course Sonia was at Bianca's second wedding to Ricky Butcher – with Carol, Robbie and Billie – as part of the show's twenty-fifth anniversary in 2010.

There were high and low points during these years as a jobbing actress and TV personality. I started going out with someone I was touring with, and we had a really lovely time together. But he was a lot older than me, by about fifteen years, and I remember him saying, 'This isn't going to work.'

I didn't believe him, swept along with it all, so I dismissed his worries by saying, 'Oh, it will.'

And then, bless him, he was right, because a year later, I found myself saying, 'Oh no, you're a bit too old for me.'

He was such a nice man, and it was a really fun year. We were playing a couple in the show, and so we had a lot of laughs together. Sometimes you find that if you're in a bubble with people for that long, it can easily happen, if you're free and single and enjoying the world, as we were. I think that's what happened. You're in your own little world together and you're away from home, travelling around the UK, and going to different places, and everything is like a lovely dream – but then you get back to normality, and it doesn't quite work.

I went through some very public personal troubles when I was in my twenties. There were periods where I was drinking too much, partying too much; I was lost and in one of those messy relationships where you break things off and then try to give it another go, and back and forth and on and on, because you don't want to give up. We kept trying until I realised that I was just letting complete chaos into my life. I tried to hide a lot of what was going on for me because I just felt so terribly ashamed of it all. But you can only hide things up to a point before the people close to you realise what's going on, and I was so lucky to have the support of my nieces to get me through that difficult time.

Sometimes, I think that the only good thing that happened during that time was Eliza, who was born in September 2010.

She was my star in the darkness, and having her gave me a reason to get back on track.

These days, I like staying in. I love being at home with Marc, Eliza and Joanie, and for a while, it made me feel panicked if someone said, 'We're all going out tonight. Come too!'

I'd think, 'Oh no, I'll have to pretend to be ill,' and start making up excuses. But I'm more confident in my choices now. Now, I know it's absolutely fine to be honest and say, 'No thank you, I don't want to go.' Even on a Thursday!

Halloween

I'm not a massive fan of Halloween, but I do really love seeing the kids out. At that time of year, it's almost pitch-black at five, so we can get out quite early once Joanie and Eliza are home from school. Our village is very, very dark, and you see all the little ones walking along with head torches on, wearing costumes and carrying little pumpkins. Everybody makes a real effort round our way, which is fun.

I wonder if anyone still plays Bloody Mary, the awful horror game me and my friends used to play on Halloween? According to the rules, you're supposed to go into a dark room with a mirror, shut the door, light a candle and turn off the light. You must be alone. Now it's time to call the ghost of Bloody Mary: stand in front of a mirror and say, 'Bloody Mary' three times. Look behind you – is 'she' there?

I found it petrifying. It got to a point where you only had to see a mirror on Halloween for someone to push you in front of it and you'd have to say 'Bloody Mary' three times. I'm not sure what I was expecting and obviously 'she' was never there, but it was terrifying all the same.

I suppose my only problem with Halloween now is that I'd rather stay in to give out the sweets and be at home for people when they knock on the door. When you go out, you're missing seeing everybody else, and it's always so nice seeing groups of kids coming up the path all dressed up, especially if you've got a really horrific mask you can wear to scare the ones that are old enough!

One of my masks is an old man with long white hair. I open the front door and peek round looking ghastly, and Marc will peer through the window wearing something equally horrific. We'll have scary carved pumpkins and giant spider webs around the door; I'll put a speaker outside with some spooky music on and it's just lots of fun. I like anything that has a community feel and brings everyone together. Come to think of it, maybe I am a fan of Halloween after all!

All Hallow's Eve on 31 October is traditionally a day for remembering the dead, and somewhere along the line, it became a light-hearted horror fest with sweets galore. In Britain, it was a Christian festival for more than a thousand years, but there are all kinds of ancient and possibly pagan rituals surrounding it: lighting fires, cracking nuts, bell-ringing and visiting your neighbours wearing a horse's skull on your head. Who knew?

If you come to our village on Halloween, you will very much see traces of the past in the way we celebrate it now. Centuries ago, people went through the streets knocking on doors and receiving soul cakes – spiced shortbread biscuits – in return for praying for the householders and their deceased relatives, particularly the ones who might only have made it halfway to heaven (which was a thing back then – you could get stuck between earth and paradise in Purgatory and spend an eternity going through purification for your venial sins. Nightmare!). Children were often deployed to collect the soul cakes and sometimes they went in disguise, or dressed like ghosts, which were believed to be the walking spirits of people stuck in Purgatory, carrying lanterns made from hollowed out turnips, known as 'jack-o'-lanterns'. Sound familiar?

Late October is the peak of apple-picking season, and I distinctly remember apple bobbing as a kid. I'll still grab a large bucket out of the shed, fill it with water and apples, and we'll bob apples with my great-nieces and nephews. My little Alfie (Marie's eldest) was so excited the first time he got to play – it just goes to show that the old-fashioned games are still alive and well.

We also played swinging apples when I was a kid, where you have to take a bite out of an apple that's hanging from the ceiling without using your hands. If you've never played it, I highly recommend it – nothing will give you the giggles like watching the kids (and the grown-ups!) desperately trying to get a bite out of an apple that keeps moving away!

Telling ghost stories was another Halloween tradition: sitting in a circle, passing a torch around and lighting up your face from below like a ghoul when it gets to your turn.

Somewhere along the line, we seem to have lost the idea of using Halloween to remember loved ones who have passed, which I think is a bit of a pity. The Mexican Day of the Dead looks like a really special celebration in the depictions I've seen in films and on TV. It takes place around the same time as Halloween, sometime between 31 October and 6 November, and its meaning is far more personal and emotional than Halloween. It's a festival, so there's a party atmosphere to it, but the focus is very much on paying respects to loved ones, friends and family members who have passed away. People make little shrines to the people they want to honour and remember, putting out photos and little things to remind them of them, from the sweets or flowers they liked to a special piece of their jewellery. It's not necessarily a day of grieving, but it can be.

Grief is a funny thing, isn't it? I find that it sometimes hits you totally unexpectedly. I can be absolutely fine for ages, and then I'll wander into M&S and see the Madagascan king prawns that I used to treat Dad to, and I'll suddenly have a tear in my eye just from looking at something I used to buy him.

I'm not sure what I believe about the afterlife. Like a lot of people, I have a vague sense of people's souls continuing after their bodies have stopped working, and of my close relatives watching over me, like guardian angels. It's not something we can ever know for certain, and yet I think as humans, regardless of our beliefs, there's a collective sense around the world of a life or an existence beyond this one.

Fifth of November

Bonfire Night reminds me of my childhood; of my dad working in the newsagents, and each year, him saying, 'I'm not bringing any fireworks home,' and me begging him, 'Please, Dad, please, please, Daddy!' He'd always give in and bring me home a box of fireworks from the shop. Then, after dinner, me and Mum and Dad would get all wrapped up in our scarves and coats and hats before going outside and lighting the first sparkler. It was just us – my brothers were grown up and gone by the time I was seven or eight – but it was such a nice evening, and I treasure those memories now.

Remember, Remember

In amongst the fireworks going off from what seems like the beginning of October, it can be easy to forget what a big deal the Gunpowder Plot was. If the thirty-six barrels of explosives found under the House of Lords on 5 November 1605 had been detonated, they would have blown up half of London, and King James I with it.

The plot was masterminded by Robert Catesby, the son of Sir William Catesby, but for some reason, we don't burn his effigy on Bonfire Night. Possibly this is because Guy, or

Guido, Fawkes was the man found guarding the gunpowder when the plot was exposed. And, while Catesby was shot and killed while on the run soon afterwards, Fawkes, as every school kid knows, was hung, drawn and quartered in the grisliest of ways. Catesby was then dug up and decapitated after his death, and his severed head was put on a spike outside the Houses of Parliament, as a warning to would-be traitors. But even that wasn't enough to ensure him lasting infamy as the biggest terrorist who never was – Guy Fawkes, for better or worse, won that contest.

I've been to big events on Fireworks Night, with hot dogs, rides and a display set to music, and we've done our own thing in our garden at home where I've made jacket potatoes and chilli for everyone. I like it best when it falls over the weekend – then it's a great excuse for a get-together – and any excuse will do, let's be honest! Nowadays, the school in our village will do something, which is great, and everyone goes to that. It has become a bit of a thing we do each year now, and I love it because it's another chance for our little community to come together.

I read the other day that your ashes can be put into fireworks, which I think is a great idea. Imagine! Everyone has a party, they're all gathered round, then someone strikes a match, and up you go! Another option is to put your ashes in a timer so that you can still be around at board game nights. I sent this information to Ellia and Maria, my nieces, because we love playing board games together. 'Here we go,'

I said. 'Keep a note.' I love the idea of my ashes being put in a board game timer, so when they're playing Scattergories or Articulate, I'm still on the table!

Chapter Seven

Friday

Monday's child is fair of face,
Tuesday's child is full of grace.
Wednesday's child is full of woe,
Thursday's child has far to go.
Friday's child is loving and giving,
Saturday's child works hard for a living.
But the child that is born on Sabbath day,
Is bonny and blithe, good and gay.

'Friday's child is loving and giving,' according to the nursery rhyme. Well, that's very nice – I was born on a Friday!

It's true that I like to make people happy; I'm a carer and a gift-giver, so you're probably not going to leave our house empty-handed if you come round for a visit. I know I take after my mum in that regard – I'm always pressing things on people as they're walking out the door. It could be any little thing: a bag of Marc's homegrown tomatoes; a tin or a bottle you've admired; a hand wash I've bought two of, by mistake;

a blouse you like that I don't wear anymore; a surprise birth-day present. 'No, take it, please. You're welcome!'

Friday is a love day, named for Frigg, the kickass Norse Venus, the goddess of all the good things: love, beauty, pleasure, sex, desire, fertility and victory. It's a good day to be born. I'm happy with it. And not only does Venus rule my birthday, but she also rules the second sign of the Zodiac, Taurus, the sign I was born under.

Me and Venus, we are peas in a pod!

But there's a drawback. A big one: I was born on a Friday the 13th, which in many cultures is thought of as an unlucky day. I can even remember Mum saying to me once, during a big argument, 'Having you was my bad luck!'

I must have done something really awful to make her say that . . . sorry, Mum.

It doesn't seem fair to consider Friday the 13th unlucky, though, because in pagan times Friday was a good day, associated with love and fertility. The number 13 was also good, and similarly linked with fertility through the lunar and menstrual cycles. So, once upon a time, Friday the 13th used to be a great day. But at some point, the tide turned and suddenly it wasn't so great, maybe because of the Christian belief that the crucifixion of Jesus happened on a Friday.

I always liked the tradition of having fish and chips at school on a Friday. Joanie and Eliza still do it at their schools, and I'm pleased to see that carrying on.

Superstition is influenced by culture, and if some people have thirteen guests for dinner, they'll set another place to offset the bad luck. This is another idea that goes back through the ages in Western culture. There's a Norse myth about Loki, the god of mischief, being the uninvited thirteenth guest at a feast where he tricked another guest into killing the god of light. In the New Testament of the Bible, Judas is the thirteenth guest at the Last Supper. And in the *Sleeping Beauty* tale, it's the thirteenth fairy who curses the baby princess Aurora. Other cultures think differently, of course; for instance, in Islam, no numbers are considered unlucky, and in many parts of China, thirteen is thought to be an auspicious number!

In the Western world, though, where it seems that absolutely loads of people have been struck by lightning, lost all their money or died in freakishly unlucky circumstances on Friday the 13th, the twelve slasher movies in the *Friday the 13th* film franchise have added to our general wariness of the date. Are they making a thirteenth, I wonder? Never mind the fact that the majority of people survive Friday the 13th completely unscathed!

You can't really be superstitious about Friday the 13th if it's your birthday, can you? It was actually an incredibly lucky day for me, considering the 400 trillion to one chance that I made it here at all. So, I've decided I'm reclaiming it and rebranding it!

I know that it's a real privilege to be getting older, especially when I think of the people who don't get that opportunity. One of my best friends in the village has a daughter who has been dealing with neuroblastoma, a type of cancer, for over four years; she's nine and doing really well, which is marvellous, but over the period that she's been poorly, I've been more involved with charity work for neuroblastoma and the children affected by it. You can't help it; you're looking at the ages and stages and I've seen maybe eight or nine children pass, all under the age of seven. Heartbreaking.

Last year, I went to the wedding of a man in his thirties who had terminal cancer. I think your day is up when it's up; you are lucky or you're unlucky, and age doesn't really come into it. That's why it's so important to live life to the full. You don't know when you're going to die, so you've just got to have a really great time for the time that you do have.

I constantly think, 'How lucky am I? I'm forty-two!' And I really am grateful to be here.

Brain Teaser #1

Do you ever think, 'What if our lives are mapped out for us by the invisible hand of fate? What if everything is pre-destined, even this thought I'm having now?'

How much difference would it make if we knew the answer to that question? On the one hand, it would drive you mad, wouldn't it, if you knew that you had no control over what you were doing? On the other hand, whether it's fate or free will dictating that you get out of bed in the morning, you've still got to do it – otherwise you won't get to the kitchen to put the kettle on and have your morning cuppa. And then where would you be?

In my mind, life seems too unpredictable to be controlled by fate, although I suppose that could be an illusion too. Maybe we've all been hypnotised to think life isn't preordained, when it actually is. In which case, does it matter?

Possibly not, to be fair!

If I had more time, I'd definitely get more into astrology. The little I do know is that my sun and moon on my astrological chart are both in Taurus, and Taureans are very down to earth, caring, loving, loyal and family-oriented. So, I'm thinking, if you are Taurus times two, your ego is never going to get you, is it? You're always going to have your feet on the ground – and that's me.

It's very literal in my case – I sometimes feel a bit uncomfortable when my feet aren't actually on the ground. I'm fine up the Shard with a glass of champagne, height-wise, and I didn't get vertigo on the London Eye. That said, I can't ride a bike to save my life, although my dad did try and teach me when I was little. Mum and Dad got me a pink Barbie bike, and one summer I pedalled madly up and down the pavement in front of our house in Dagmar Terrace with stabilisers on. Maybe the stabilisers came off for a bit – I can't remember – but ultimately, it wasn't really my thing, and we never went for bike rides as a family, so I didn't get another bike.

Ten years later, I was in the green room at work – I must have been about seventeen – and Adam Woodyatt, who plays Ian Beale in *EastEnders*, said, 'I'm organising a charity bike ride from Albert Square to Weatherfield; *EastEnders* to *Coronation Street*. Will you sign up?'

'Yes, I'll do it,' I said. 'That'd be great. Brilliant.'

Adam grinned. 'The bicycles are amazing – come and see them.' He led me to a big room that we used to call 'the tennis court', because it looked like an old PE assembly hall. A delivery of bikes had just arrived, and they were so ultra lightweight that you could pick them up with one finger. He was so delighted with them. I confidently got on one to have a go – and instantly fell down flat in a Lee Evans-style pratfall! I was so embarrassed that I've never got on a bike again, and I never made it to Weatherfield!

They say you never forget how to ride a bike, but I can't do it – and now, when I think about it, I've never been able to roller skate or ice skate either. People will say, 'Put the ice skates on. You can have a go.' But I can't even stand up in them!

Although I haven't been tested, I'm pretty sure I have dyspraxia, which is quite a common coordination disorder. In my case, it's definitely a problem with balance. When I come down a high staircase, I have to concentrate really hard and hold the handrail because I think I'm going to fall. Even when I'm getting on an escalator at a train station, I have to take a deep breath and psych myself up. I like it much better when I've got my feet firmly on the ground. Although when I'm walking along a cliff in Cornwall, my legs do sometimes go a bit too.

The only other thing I know about Taureans is that they are quite materialistic, unfortunately. And that's true of me, even if I like to pretend it's not. I love nice things and I'm a sucker for a label. I like a posh candle. I enjoy going into a designer shop and getting a pair of shoesor a fancy handbag. It is shallow, but I enjoy it, not gonna lie.

Astrology is one thing, but I'm not so comfortable with something like spiritualism. My friend's mum was a psychic, and the first time I met her she asked, 'Do you get tired a lot?'

Although I'm permanently on the go, sometimes I do get very drained and tired, which I told her. 'No wonder,' she said. 'You've got so many spirits around you. They're following you around, talking to you and asking for help. That uses a lot of energy.'

Whether or not there was any truth in this, and I have no idea either way, it wasn't something I wanted to explore. I like to think that the souls of our loved ones are in the ether somewhere and they're looking out for us – and that's as far as I want to go into it. I'm a bit of a scaredy-cat in that way!

It's funny what does and doesn't appeal. Despite what I've just said about spiritualism, I am quite drawn to mysticism – I bought my first pack of Tarot cards when I was about eleven. I can't even remember now why or how I got into it, but I went into the astrology shop in Covent Garden and asked for some Tarots, which came wrapped in black silk, with a book on how to read them. Back home, I tried to memorise the meaning of the cards, and then I went through a phase of doing Tarot readings for my cousins and friends.

We all loved it, but in time, like most teenage phases, I put the cards to one side and moved on.

Fast forward a couple of decades and Joanie loves crystals. Whenever we go to the seaside, we'll go into a shop and pick a crystal. Last year, I took her to that same shop in Covent Garden where I'd bought the Tarot cards all those years ago. 'When Mummy lived in Islington, I used to get the bus here to buy crystals and things,' I told her.

To my astonishment, the shopkeeper was the same man who'd been there when I was a kid. I walked up to the counter and said, 'Your Tarot cards . . .'

'I know what you're going to say,' he cut in, 'because I remember you buying yours.'

Well, that was unexpected! 'You haven't got the same ones you had thirty years ago, have you?' I asked, trying not to look too surprised. 'I'd like to buy them again.'

He went down to the stock room, found the exact same packet and I bought them! They're not open yet, but when I've got a bit more time, I'm going to get them out and start doing my readings again.

I'd also like to explore astrology more – and planetary influences. I've been taking more notice of the universe these last few years, especially the moon. I think it's natural when you're at a crossroads in life to maybe look further afield for inspiration and guidance, and I became interested in 'moonology' during a time when I was in turmoil about my direction in life.

Hitting that milestone fortieth birthday had focused my

mind on what I really wanted from my life and career, and I'd decided that I'd really like a change. Having these feelings happened to coincide with being asked to be a guest on a couple of podcasts: *Comfort Eating* with Grace Dent was one of the first and it was brilliant; I really enjoyed meeting Grace and chatting about my food memories. Then the comedian and actor Joe Wilkinson got in touch and we started talking. Joe does a podcast with the actor and comedian David Earl, and they invited me on. It's called *Chatabix* and we had an absolute blast, and soon they invited me back again.

After my niece Maria planted the seed in my mind that I should start doing my own podcast, I began to think about how it could work. 'Could I really start something on my own?' I didn't have any experience in starting a podcast. On the one hand, I knew how oversaturated the podcast world is. There are thousands of podcasts competing for attention. Why would people choose to listen to mine? And, on a practical level, I had to wonder, 'Financially, is there any gain in it?'

On the other hand, I had a such good laugh with David and Joe whenever I went on the *Chatabix* podcast that I knew in my gut it was something I wanted to do. I had so many thoughts whirring round my head: 'Maybe I should just stick to what I know,' I kept thinking. 'Keep small, stay where I am and do what I'm known for doing.'

It was a real moment of clarity when I thought, 'No, I really do want to do a podcast. Why can't I do that?'

It wasn't easy, because working at *EastEnders* comes with a lot of contractual rules that mean there aren't many opportunities outside of the job. That's how the BBC works, and it's absolutely fine if you are happy to accept the rules and go along with the parameters of the job, which in most cases you're very grateful for. It is also okay to want more in life, though, and I've learned with these things that you shouldn't feel embarrassed about it, as if you're asking too much.

Still, I had a big old internal fight with myself before I was brave enough to approach my bosses at the BBC to discuss starting a podcast. It was scary. I had a real fire in my belly, though. It was a passion project and I knew I had to find the courage. At last, I did it – I arranged a meeting.

'I really want to make this work. Can we talk about it?' I asked. 'I don't think it will affect my job or my role. It has nothing to do with Sonia; I'm not going to talk about *EastEnders* or about Sonia.'

I needed to reassure them that it wouldn't get in the way of my work at *EastEnders*. After all, nothing ever has; I've always been very professional. And I wanted them to know that I wasn't suddenly going to start coming in late, or become unfocused on the day job. I wasn't going to let it interfere with my BBC work, so there was no conflict.

It was very nice to have the trust my bosses at the BBC then gave me. They understood that the podcast would give me the opportunity to start branching out, and, when I asked for an unpaid break, they gave me that space to get the pod up and running. So now I had the chance to test the water.

I wasn't thinking of leaving *EastEnders* when I started developing *Life with Nat*. I knew I could do it on top of my work there and so it seemed a great option. The joy of recording a podcast is that it's something I can squeeze in whenever I can. My studio is upstairs in my house, so, whilst I might have a really busy week, that's just my tough luck and I can just pop up to the studio and record it at ten o'clock at night once the girls are in bed, if needs must.

'Let's give it a go and see how it goes,' I thought.

In my head, I had really started to focus on the idea of a podcast community, setting up a specific WhatsApp number and getting to chat to real people. From other podcasts I'd listened to, it didn't seem like something that many people were doing, and I had a strong sense that it was going to work. As much as I like acting – and I do really love acting – I also like my time at home, which podcasting would give me more of. I also knew there was so much more I wanted to do and was capable of.

I'd already built a community on social media, on Instagram especially, doing my own videos and just getting to be me, Nat – not playing any role or character. That's where it really started, on Instagram, when I realised that people were interested in me – the everyday, mundane stuff. Fans and followers seemed to like the fact that I'm so normal – whatever normal is! – despite being on the telly for so many years.

Having a following on Instagram gave me confidence for the pod, and from there, other things started to happen. I think the podcast gave people the chance to hear who I really am – and people hadn't really heard that before, apart from short little snippets.

Other projects began to come my way, and after a while, as opportunities started to mount up, I began thinking about leaving *EastEnders*. It certainly wasn't a straightforward decision though, and I went through a lot of internal struggles over it. I mean, why would you walk away from a job you love that pays you a regular wage and gives you a fantastic sense of security? I thought, 'What if it doesn't work out?'

At the time, I was reading a book about the moon that really resonated with me. 'What's that got to do with the podcast?' I hear you ask.

Well, the central idea of Moonology is that the phases and cycles of the moon can affect our mood and energy levels. Once you break them down, the moon's phases and cycles can provide a useful framework for exploring your emotions, as well as helping pinpoint what you really want from life and how to get it.

I found it helpful to write down new objectives with every new moon. Then, I'd check in on them over the eight phases of every lunar cycle, from crescent to full moon. It was a way of being mindful, and it created a system for building the courage to make the changes I wanted to see in my life, step by step. One month, my objective might be to be brave and set my intention; the following month, it was to tell people about that intention; the next, to act on it, and so on and so forth.

It's not that I followed a black and white plan – it wasn't that straightforward, but I did feel as if this connection to astrology and the moon was helping to nudge me forward and push boundaries.

People can be cynical about the influence of the sun, moon and stars in our lives, but it's quite ridiculous to think that there isn't a link. The moon's gravity literally holds the Earth in place – without it, the Earth might not tilt, and if the Earth didn't tilt, there would be no seasons. You only need to look at how the moon's gravitational pull affects the seas and the tides: it's only a sixth of the Earth's gravity, but that's enough to tug at our oceans when they are closest to the moon, causing them to swell and give rise to high tides. As our bodies are comprised of eighty per cent water, it shouldn't be surprising to think that the moon probably has an impact on us, too – but how can we define it?

The belief that the moon's phases affect our behaviour goes back to ancient times. An early werewolf myth was written down thousands of years ago in *The Epic of Gilgamesh*, the oldest surviving literary work. The idea that people go mad or become lunatics at the full moon grew from there. Is there a causal link between crime and the full moon? No one seems to be absolutely sure. It's one of those things that people can feel in their bones, but isn't scientifically proven, like the link between bad weather and arthritis. My nan used to swear down that her joints ached a lot more when it was raining. She could even predict the rain when she felt certain arthritic twinges. But scientists can't find any evidence of a direct connection between our behaviour and the moon, so who knows?

After following a simple plan to move forward with my intentions, there came a point when the full moon was in Leo, exactly when my chart had predicted that I would reap rewards from the groundwork I'd been putting in to make changes to my life. No word of a lie, it came true – and it all happened on one day. In the morning, I was given the green light for a BBC documentary that I'd proposed a year earlier, and in the afternoon, another two job offers came in. I politely declined them, but it was still amazing to see the fruits of my labour.

It felt as if I was on a roll, and I decided to take advantage of it. 'All this is happening today,' I thought, 'so I'm also going to message a company I really love and tell them I'd like to work with them.'

So, I grabbed the bull by the horns and messaged them – and they got straight back to me and said, 'We would love to meet you!' That would never have happened if I hadn't been proactive and reached out.

What I'm saying isn't really about the moon's influence – or rather, it's not *just* about that – although I'm certain there's a connection there that everybody could feel if they tapped into it. It's actually more about believing that you can make things happen for yourself, if you have intentions and if you're brave enough to put yourself out there.

I truly believe that you can make your own luck, so don't be scared to say to people, 'I'd love to try . . .' or 'I'd really like . . .' or 'I'm interested in . . .' It's a way of opening yourself up to opportunity.

A couple of years ago, I started looking into the idea that you can manifest your desires through focused thoughts, self-belief and action. Now, I realise that I must have been manifesting for years and years, or at least for as long as I've been telling people: 'I love Ricky Gervais. I will work with Ricky Gervais one day.'

It always made everyone laugh. Not in a horrible way, but I think they were probably a bit perplexed. I imagine that hearing me say that made them think, 'Is that something you could actually do, though, Nat?'

Then I started going on Joe and David's *Chatabix* podcast – and, being in the comedy world, they knew Ricky Gervais. So, of course, whenever they mentioned him, I'd say, 'I'm such a big fan. I'd love to work with him.'

Then, one day in 2024, Ricky Gervais phoned me up and said, 'Do you want to be a cat in my animation?'

Is that the power of manifesting? For me it was just so amazing that I got to be in a room with Ricky Gervais for two whole days!

I was a bag of nerves on the first day of the job, but I tried to play it cool over breakfast with David Earl, who was also working on it. I brushed off the idea of feeling nervous.

'How are you feeling about this?' he asked me.

'I've been so busy that I haven't had time to think about it,' I said. Now, that was a flat-out lie! In truth, I'd been thinking of nothing else for days.

It is very difficult to meet someone you've admired for a long time. I've grown up with Ricky Gervais: I've watched his programmes, seen him live, and listened to him on the radio. Honestly? I'm a little bit obsessed with him. So, I felt like a competition winner when I finally got the chance to meet him. Still, I tried to keep my head and stay professional, and I think it went very well. The job was over two days, a few hours a day, and it felt extremely surreal to be sat in a room with him and some of his regular actors. I was pleased with my performance. It was an interesting one because the pictures were going to be drawn after we'd done the voices, so we had quite a lot of freedom with it. I played his mum at one point (as a cat!) and I think he enjoyed the whole thing as much as I did. That's the best you can do – leave hoping that the boss is happy – and I think he was. Maybe that's it now for me and Ricky, and my small window to meet him has closed, but deep down, I don't believe it's finished. I still feel like I'm going to work with him again in some way.

I remember being asked to do an appearance on a TV show once, and somebody said to me, 'You wouldn't have got that opportunity if you weren't already in *EastEnders*.'

My brother David couldn't believe it. 'That's crazy!' he said. 'That would be like my maths teacher from primary school saying that I've only become a bank manager because he taught me how to count!'

You get breaks, yes, but after that, it's up to you to keep your job. You have to be professional. You have to be nice to people. Otherwise, you could blow your chances and end up back where you started with nothing to show for it.

I often find myself mentally returning to the day I went into

Anna Scher's acting classes for the first time as a working-class kid from London. At Anna's, it didn't matter where you were from, who you were, who your mum and dad were, or the jobs anyone did. You just went into a room and did the best you could, and that was your opportunity.

I'm currently trying to manifest an appearance on the Channel 4 show, *Taskmaster*, which I love. I send the producer a message every three or four months to say I'd like to be on the show. My last one was just a line saying, 'I'm not going to give up. I hope you're well. I'd love to try out for *Taskmaster*.'

'Great to hear from you. Never give up!' he replied.

Obviously, there's a balance, and you don't want to be seen to be hassling people or driving them mad bothering them, but I also don't think you can ever aim too high. You should never feel that you're not enough to do those things. With *Taskmaster*, the worst that could happen is that the producer stops emailing me back. If that were to happen, at least I'd know that I'd tried absolutely.

West End theatre is something else I would love to do – flex those stage acting chops again. It would be a dream come true to make my way into Central London and do a little play of some sort. We'll see what happens!

Reading this, you might think, 'Nat's been famous for ages so she doesn't have to worry about money – it's all right for her.'

But what I'm saying has nothing to do with money, really. It's about connections with people and telling them how you feel. Maybe you work in a bank and feel low, or someone's upsetting you at work, or you've got three jobs because you've got to keep a roof over your head and you're a single parent. Whatever your situation, if you're unhappy with things, it's worth having a think about how you could go about making changes.

Someone with three jobs might be so busy that they never get the chance to say out loud, 'I'd love to consolidate my work and have just one job.' But if he or she were to say that to seven people, one of those seven people might say, 'I know someone who might have something for you . . .'

It's about opening up and being brave enough to talk to people. That's not to say it can't be tiring, though. It isn't easy to keep plugging on, or to take time to think about what you want. It's also quite daunting, isn't it? Sometimes it's just easier to stay in your lane and think, 'I'm doing what I'm doing and it's working, okay? So, I'll just stay here.'

I think we all understand that mentality, because life is busy and there's so much going on.

You can always take a moment to have a little check in with yourself, though, can't you? Next time you find your-self with a quiet moment – maybe just before bed, or while you're brushing your teeth, or driving to the supermarket, ask yourself, 'Am I happy? Is there anything I could be doing to improve things for myself?'

It's important to say that it's about improving stuff for *you*, mind; not just for everybody else all the time. As someone who automatically wants to care for other people, I know how easy it is for your own needs to slip and slide all the way down to the bottom of the priority pile!

Think about what you want. Put it out there. Tell a few people how you feel. And tell people you might not usually talk to and who aren't in your circle, because the people who are closest around you may not want you to change. People like familiarity. They like you to be who they think you are: 'Good old Nat is Sonia in *EastEnders* – that's what she does.'

Yet, in my experience, once you branch out and start doing other things, people often really like it. I've had so many positive comments about the projects I've taken on outside of *EastEnders*, even the ones where I've stepped right out of my comfort zone and felt utterly terrified as I did them.

There aren't many people in soaps who have crafted a career where they're known for both their character and themselves, and I feel pleased that I have managed to do that continually over the years. Back in the day, typecasting was so prevalent that if you did one thing in the industry, that was it, whereas now, you have Hollywood actors doing telly, adverts, or music; creatively, things have really crossed over.

Podcasting is a medium where I get to have my cake and eat it too: I can be creative and do something I really love doing, at home. I really like to be in control – and the podcasts allow me that. Marc and I also really enjoy doing podcasts together. It's like a shared interest, something the two of us get to do. We're really invested in it.

Marc said it the other night: 'You had an idea and it's

amazing what you're achieving. Look at what you're learning out of it!'

He's right, and it was lovely of him to point it out, because when you're in the moment, you can forget sometimes to take stock of what you have achieved. I feel proud that I've done it all by myself. The podcast is my creation. I've never achieved anything like it before. It's my thing that I've done: I've set up my studio at home; I've come up with the ideas for themes and guests and the people who do it with me and have become a part of it all. It's family-orientated, which I love. The whole thing is truly amazing, honestly. I feel really grateful, and in my wildest dreams I never imagined it going this well.

It's why I always say to people: 'If you have something that you keep thinking you want to do, you must act on it. You must do it.'

*

I don't often go out on a Friday, but me and Marc will always pop something on the telly, and it will often be comedy. I love *Live at the Apollo*; I'm in absolute awe of stand-up comedians. It takes a certain kind of bravery to stand up in front of an audience and tell jokes – and I honestly don't think I could do it. I'd like to do more live work, though, and I've been dipping my toe in at small events, so you never know. Maybe a live podcast would come first. I think I could do that without becoming too nervous!

My leaning towards comedy has always been in me. It came

out in performance when I used to entertain the old people up at the hospital when I was eight visiting my nans, and at various moments playing Sonia, from her trumpet-playing days onwards. Outside of *EastEnders*, I've done quite a few comic cameos over the years, starting with the BBC Two comedy series *Psychoville* in 2009, where I got to appear alongside Dawn French and Eileen Atkins. That was exciting, as I absolutely adore Dawn French. She's a comedy genius and I still love *The Vicar of Dibley* to this day. Jennifer Saunders, as well, and Victoria Wood and Julie Walters – all the funny women I grew up watching. It felt as if comedy was very male-orientated in the 1980s and early 1990s, and it's great that they changed the landscape.

I absolutely loved appearing in the third series of the BBC sitcom *Motherland* in 2021, playing an uptight assistant teacher. I got on really well with Diane Morgan, who plays one of the mums, and she asked me to do a cameo when her BBC series *Mandy* came along. I played a gangster in *Mandy* and really enjoyed it. I'd like a bit more of that, I think. More recently, I guest-starred in the BBC Three series *Boarders*, playing another teacher – an eccentric maths teacher! That really was fun.

Humour Corner

My dad always said sarcasm was the lowest form of wit and that's stuck with me. It's nice to have a joke, but not by putting other people down. I like humour that skewers pretensions, not people.

My final day at *EastEnders* was a Friday, which was fitting, really. End of the week, take a deep breath – and the weekend begins, along with a whole new career change! Phew!

Before I got to the point of leaving the show, though, I had a mountain to climb. We were doing a live episode as part of the show's fortieth anniversary celebrations, and I was absolutely petrified. It wasn't just the fear of things going wrong in front of millions of viewers, or of any mistakes being posted online and staying there forever; I was also wondering what would be in store for Sonia, because anything can happen in a live episode, and being *EastEnders*, they usually involve accidents, fires, crimes and multiple deaths. The date was set for 20 February 2025, exactly when I was going to be playing out my final days as Sonia before I left the show. *Would Sonia be killed off?*

When I had a meeting with my boss Chris Clenshaw to discuss the episode, I was thinking, 'I could be for the chop here.'

The scriptwriters could easily have thought, 'Nat wants to go. Let's kill Sonia off and make it a big story for the fortieth.'

So, I was really pleased and happy when Chris said that they would be leaving the door open for Sonia to come back, if I ever wanted to. It felt like a testament to Sonia, and to me. They wanted it to be a dramatic episode for her, but the script was also going to celebrate all that she's been through over the decades, and she was going to give birth in the rubble of the Queen Vic, after a car crashes into the building and causes an explosion. It was a really satisfying way for Sonia's life on the show to come full circle, twenty-five years on from giving birth to Chloe on the sofa in the Jackson family lounge at the age of fifteen.

Even lovelier for me, Chris said that they wanted my voice to overlay the closing scenes of the episode. I felt it was a real privilege and I cried when he told me, as it was always June Brown's character Dot Cotton that used to do the voiceovers.

'Am I doing the right thing in leaving?' I asked myself, suddenly feeling wobbly about my decision.

It was reassuring to know I was well thought of, but in my heart, I knew it was time to move on. If you're somewhere for a very long time, you can become complacent about how special it is. You don't want to become moany, you don't want to become stale, and you can't let anything define you by staying too long. It was totally fine and all too natural to have had that wobble; it's testament to how much I've loved working on *EastEnders*. I just needed to remind myself that it was a real privilege to be leaving on such a high.

The rehearsal for the live episode lasted for ten days, which doesn't sound long, but in reality, it feels like ages for soap actors because we're used to getting through scenes really fast. We needed the time, though, because the jeopardy of live television means there are a lot of nuts and bolts to work out before you even get onto thinking about your performance. For instance, if Sonia was going to be giving birth, we had to work out how to get rid of her pregnancy bump after the baby had arrived without viewers seeing the prosthetic bump slip out!

It was a brilliant ten days. For once, we were an ensemble,

all working together. It almost felt like a different job. We weren't speeding through fourteen scenes a day; we were concentrating on one half-hour episode, rehearsing together each day to get it absolutely spot-on. It was like doing theatre but on the telly, and that's rare these days, so it felt special. To have the honour of doing the voiceover at the end made it even more so, for me.

But on the Monday of rehearsals, with three days to go until the show, I became rather obsessive about the performance side of it. I was starting to panic, I think, after spending so long working out the mechanics of what I'd be doing. Now, all I wanted was to throw myself into the drama. 'I've really got to go for it to see where I want to take it,' I thought.

So, there I was on the floor squeezing out this fake baby. We were doing it as a live run-through, and I was really getting carried away in the moment. Suddenly, I heard a pop in my chest area. It was the weirdest thing, and in that moment, I had one of those out of body experiences when you can see yourself from above. I looked down on myself and thought, 'Why are you overdoing it? That's a stupid thing to be doing.'

I didn't know what I'd done to myself, only that it was bad, and then whatever it was that had popped out seemed to pop back into place. As I wasn't feeling much pain, I carried on with the rehearsal right up until the end monologue, but afterwards, I felt a bit sore and knew that something wasn't quite right.

I saw a studio medic, and they asked me, 'Can you lift

your arm; can you stretch?' I did it all and they said, 'Well, you seem okay.'

Tuesday came, and I was in a lot of pain when I woke up. 'I don't know what I've done, but something isn't right,' I said to Marc.

'You need to get an X-ray and see a doctor,' he insisted.

I had rehearsals on the Tuesday and didn't have time to fit in a doctor's visit, so I soldiered on, hoping it would go away on its own, but the pain was so bad that by Wednesday morning I thought, 'I really need to go somewhere now.' So, to my relief, my lovely company manager organised a taxi and a private X-ray – it turned out that with all that pushing, I had fractured my sternum. All by overdoing it as I pretended to give birth! Disaster!

Suddenly, I couldn't vacuum or make the bed. Anyone who knows me knows what an absolute nightmare that was! What was really frustrating was that I'd be absolutely fine one minute and then I'd do a small movement, and I'd be in agony. Marc kept telling me off and reminded me it would never get better if I didn't rest. After that, all I could do was potter around the kitchen making a lasagna, and even that was too much after a while. Unfortunately, there's no treatment for a fractured sternum. It's like a broken rib. You just have to take painkillers and wait for it to heal.

Suddenly, it was Thursday, and the countdown began to the fortieth anniversary live episode of *EastEnders*. One thing I really hate about doing a live episode is that sense you have that people are just waiting for you to make a mistake or forget a line – almost as if they're hoping to catch you out. If the worst does happen, you know it will end up online and you'll never be able to forget it. It's different when you're doing theatre. The live aspect is just as exciting, but if one of the actors gets something wrong, there might be a gasp in the audience and then that's the end of it. It doesn't go on social media to haunt you.

Incredibly, there were no mistakes on the day. In fact, I think most of the viewers were probably thinking, 'Was this actually pre-recorded?' and that's exactly what you want them to think.

It went so well that it would have been hard to top that experience. I think I would have felt a little deflated if I'd gone back into work on the Monday, business as usual, after we'd achieved that together. It was just another sign that it was the right time to leave, feeling happy.

I still had a few things to mop up after the live episode, but before I knew it, the last day had arrived and I was leaving. I felt a mix of emotions, but because I'd been deliberating on what to do for a good year, I knew deep down that I was ready to go. Still, I felt quite bad that I didn't shed a tear.

I gave a speech at my leaving do on the Friday.

'I've been at *EastEnders* on and off for thirty-two years, which is three-quarters of my life,' I said. 'So, it's not just a job for me. It's a home.'

Looking back now, it's funny, because although I love *EastEnders* with all my heart, it's also good to give it a break. I think the characters also need a break. Sonia's had a lot going on through the years. If she comes back in five or ten years' time, if that's the right thing, people will be excited to see her again and find out what she's been up to. With *EastEnders*, the plot possibilities are endless. Sonia could have got up to anything within that time!

Coincidentally, my executive producer, Chris Clenshaw, was leaving on the same day as I was, and that was nice, as we'd always had a good, honest relationship. So many lovely people came to see me off, including my friends from the costume department, Beth and Tracy, who I've worked with for years. Tracy was my dresser when I was ten, and she's still there! She gave me a beautiful picture of me as a little girl with her and Cathy, who was a dresser at the time. That's what I mean when I say it's not just a job, because you've known these people for a long time. You've seen them more than you've seen some of your own family, and it's a lot to leave behind.

I also know that leaving was a brave thing for me to do because it was a really good job, which meant it was easy to go to work, and now I was stepping into the unknown. With *EastEnders*, you get your calls each week and it's regular. I could have just carried on doing that for years. I've been there consistently for the last eleven years, apart from a break when Joanie was born, and those four months in 2024 when I started up the podcast. I could easily have stayed another decade or two, and I know I would have loved it.

Still, I'm not thinking about going back this time around. I said goodbye, and in my head, Sonia was in Dot's kitchen for the last time. It felt very final. I haven't had that feeling before with the breaks I've had, but this really felt like the end.

I don't want to think about returning to *EastEnders* because I think that will hold me back. I have to accept that that chapter of my life has ended, and now I'm moving onwards, looking forward.

Valentine's Day

I've had some lovely Valentine's Days, but I don't find it a particularly memorable day. On some Valentine's, there's been a beautiful, posh candle next to a big bunch of flowers on the table; others there's been nothing because Marc and I have been too busy with work. Sometimes we've made the effort and gone for a lovely meal in the evening; other times we've had a quick pasta pesto and an early night.

I'm not overly bothered about Valentine's Day. It's not that I don't like it; I just don't think there should be any pressure on you to celebrate it. It's fine to do nothing, and it's lovely to do something. There shouldn't be an expectation.

You can say, 'I love you' every day, and do something nice for your partner any day of the year.

There is something sweet about having a day for love, but I know that Valentine's Day can be tough for people who haven't got someone, because it's plastered all over Instagram. There are pictures of couples and promos for flowers and gifts, and 'With all my love,' swirled across everything, and in that way, it feels quite manipulative.

The best Valentine's Days are when you're in a happy relationship and you get a nice card that makes you smile. The worst are when you're a teenager – or they were for me at least, when it seemed like everyone in school got a card, and I didn't. The pressure of 'Who fancies who?' was at its highest point on Valentine's Day. I was never that girl, and I have to say, it was a bit rubbish.

This Valentine's Day, Eliza had a Galentine's night – a sleepover with the girls. What a great idea!

I messaged her while she was with her friends. *Did you get a card from anyone?*

Nope.

Well, they're still all young and boring.

#lonely, because I have no Valentines this year! she messaged back. Then she followed it up with, *No one knows what they're missing out on. I am a diva.*

She knows what's what.

The idea for Galentine's Day comes from the US sitcom *Parks and Recreation*. The main character, Leslie Knope, sees it as a chance to get together with her gal friends for the evening to celebrate female friendship and 'ovaries before broveries.' She has her Galentine's on 13 February – St Valentine's Eve – but it seems to have quite quickly slipped over to the actual day for a lot of girls and women who don't want to be defined by whether they've been sent a Valentine's card or not.

It's worth remembering that the Valentine's Day card has tragic origins. During the Roman Empire, so the story goes, St Valentine left a note to his jailer's daughter saying, 'From your Valentine' right before he was executed on 14 February. It couldn't be sadder, especially if she opened it and said, 'Ew, no thanks, mate!'

Valentine's Day sounds more fun in past centuries, when it was a game of forfeits. Equal numbers of young men and women (bachelors and maids) would get together and write their names – or made-up names – on pieces of paper that they drew by lots. The rules don't sound too rigid, but it seems that the bachelors tended to stick by the maids whose names they had drawn. They gave them little presents and treats and wore their names on their jackets or sleeves for a few days – and sometimes it led to love. It's tempting to think this is where the phrase 'heart on your sleeve' comes from, but that actually goes back to medieval jousts and knights wearing the emblem of their chosen lady on a handkerchief tied to their arm.

I do find Valentine's Day quite commercial. A bunch of roses goes up to fifty quid. Ridiculous! Going out for a nice meal suddenly doubles in price. I don't think people should feel forced into doing it. Be a bit clever, I say. Go out for dinner the following week instead.

In the past, I've felt a weight of expectation at the approach of Valentine's Day – and so often it hasn't delivered. But why do we feel compelled to make a show of feeling on a particular day, or pressure our partner into doing something that they might not feel comfortable with? I've been guilty of it, but I think with age and with sense, you realise that none of that stuff is important. It's nice to show someone you appreciate them on special occasions, but it's the day-to-day love and kindness in a relationship that really counts.

Chapter Eight

Saturday

Saturday is the best of all the days for a lot of people. It's a day of leisure and freedom, with another one to follow tomorrow. Saturday can be a day to choose what you want to do.

The day after I left *EastEnders* was a Saturday. After eleven years of never being able to colour my hair or paint my nails because it didn't fit with Sonia's look, at last I could do what I wanted. So, taking the bull by the horns, I dyed my hair red and had extensions put in! I went to the nail shop and put on lovely false nails, and had a pedicure. What a treat! I even had my eyebrows micro-bladed, so now I won't need my eyebrow pencil on that desert island. It felt freeing to do what I wanted to do without having to think of Sonia.

My hair took ten hours. Imagine! My natural colour is a very dark brunette, and my lovely hairdresser didn't want to be too harsh with it and dry it out, so she lifted it bit by bit. She did a really good job: she washed it, conditioned it and put colour in it several times. It felt like it went on forever.

She arrived at the house at half past twelve. At five thirty I said, 'I've got a podcast to do at six o'clock!'

'Well, it's not finished,' she said, 'so I'll have dinner with

Marc and the girls while you do your podcast, and we'll have to carry on after that.'

So, when six o'clock rolled around, off I went upstairs for an hour, and when I got back she started putting the extensions in. As much as I hate sitting down all day, the whole thing was fun and it did feel like a treat. I just wanted to feel good – and by the time I went to bed I felt like a whole new woman!

I don't find Saturday relaxing as a rule. Eliza's usually got a sports match during term time, so it's still like a weekday in that I still have that out-of-the-door-to-school feeling when I wake up. Sometimes I'll stay with her and watch the match, but other times, I might go home and potter before I pick her up.

I am never going to sit down and do nothing if I have a day off work. I actually find it impossible to just sit around. Being at home, for me, means a chance to get the washing done, dried, ironed, hung up and put away all on the same day. That really does make me happy, but it's not relaxing – not until it's done, anyway.

We all have our quirks, and they can vary massively. For some people, if they haven't read two books in a week, they feel disappointed in themselves, whereas for me, having three overflowing baskets of washing puts my teeth on edge. I want all of it washed, folded and put away before I can even think about meeting up with a friend. Certain other things are important to me, too: the floor being washed; my glass tables being clean. I'm like my mum was in that way: if my house is a mess, my head is a mess.

Mum was very neat, but to the point where I can sense that something wasn't quite right in her regular-as-clockwork routine and how clean the house was. It was all very regimented, and she definitely didn't like change.

A lot of people would say, 'What a waste of time! It's only dust and it'll come back in a week.'

Wasn't it the famous wit, Quentin Crisp, who said that you don't have to do any housework at all? 'After the first four years, the dirt doesn't get any worse,' he declared. 'You just have to not lose your nerve.'

But, for me, as for my mum, it's important to have everything clean and in order. I'm not completely rigid about it, though. If an opportunity arises for the children, or something comes up that we can all do together, then to hell with it – sod the dusting and let's go and have fun. But on quiet days, when there's not a lot going on, I do prioritise my chores – or at least I did until quite recently, when I was trying to fit so much into my schedule that I realised I was working seven days a week. With no break at the weekend, I was finding it mentally difficult to let go of my household tasks, which was a bit concerning. That's when I realised that I would have to start becoming less worried about keeping up appearances. As much as I love my house and pottering around doing the cleaning and keeping it nice, if you're so busy that all you can think of when you get home are the things that you need to get done around the house, something needs to change.

That moment of clarity came during the 2024 Christmas

holiday, during my final few months at *EastEnders*. 'Why am I so stressed about everything being perfect?' I wondered.

I'd be working so hard all week and then on a Saturday morning I'd be running around, sorting out all the washing and doing housework.

So, one Saturday I actually had a day of doing nothing, which really is unlike me, but I needed it. Well, I say 'doing nothing', but actually, I was playing schools with Joanie, which was really something. And it made me realise that maybe I'd been focusing too much on keeping the house in order and missing out on the important things, like playing.

There's still a part of me saying, 'This all needs to be done,' but there's also another part coming in now, saying, 'It's not going anywhere, so just enjoy your day at home, because you're back to work and really busy again next week.'

Our lovely nanny sometimes helps with the washing, and I do have a cleaner. I don't always book them because I enjoy doing everything myself, but the truth is, you can't do it all. When I'm really busy with work, I get home and want to do stuff with the children, rather than jumping up to put another load of washing on, and all the rest of it.

'Where's your phone?' Joanie asked, while we were playing schools.

'It's in the kitchen,' I said. And that is where it stayed.

Having Saturday off has become a necessity now, although if a nice job comes up on a Saturday or Sunday, then I won't turn it down. If I'm exhausted, having one day off revives me. I'm like a dead battery that needs to be recharged. I still don't want to sit around and do nothing though; I want to play with Joanie or go out with the girls. Even though I prefer it when the shops are quiet during the week, and even though I would rather stay at home on a Saturday afternoon than brave the crowds, my kids like going out shopping with me, and so that's going to be more of a Saturday thing in future.

Now that I'm around more for the girls, I would also love to go for an occasional lunch on a Saturday afternoon with Marc. It would be great to sit in a pub garden in the countryside for a few hours, just me and him, or get the train to London and soak up the weekend buzz by having a wander round Borough Market and popping to the Tate – and not sparing a thought for the heaps of washing piling up at home!

The idea of workers having a full weekend off originated in 1908, when a New England mill owner decided to shut down production on a Saturday as well as a Sunday, so that his Jewish staff could observe the Saturday Sabbath. Before long, he realised something important: his workforce was actually more productive when they had more time off. The difference was so startling that nearby businesses also started giving their staff the whole weekend off. Within a few years, mass manufacturers across America were doing the same, and in the UK, the weekend became the official policy of the Boots Corporation in 1934. It was better for business; it was better for everybody.

It just goes to show how much we need to rest – for the sake of our bodies, our brains and our minds. For our

muscles, organs, blood pressure, stress levels, immune
system, concentration, mood, creativity, energy, performance and overall quality of life . . .

I always think that Saturday gets better as the day goes on.
Marc will often be filming horse racing on a Saturday, so
he's out and about during the day. One of the reasons I think
mine and Marc's relationship has worked so well is that we
both understand what work is like for the other person, and
the fact that it's not a regular 9–5 sort of a job. Some people
say it's good to have the yin and yang of being with someone
outside the business if you're in it yourself, but for us, I think
it's worked precisely because we are both in it. We accept the
long hours, the freelancer's life, the not always knowing what
you're doing next – and that's why it still works between us.

When Marc gets home, I'll usually be in the kitchen listening to the radio and getting some bits and pieces ready for
dinner. I try and time my food prep with Liza Tarbuck's show
on BBC Radio 2. I love her show – she's a genius. Saturday is
a lovely day to do a bit of meal prep too, if you're in at about
two o'clock and you've got a few hours to kill before you start
dinner. I really think I could happily spend days in the kitchen,
cooking with the radio on. It's just my favourite thing.

I like trying new recipes when I have the time. Last year,
I wasn't sure what to do with all the chillis and tomatoes
we had left over in the garden, so, I typed in, 'What can
I make?' and up came a lovely chilli and tomato chutney. It
was a labour of love and took about three hours to make,

and I only got a jar and a half out of it, but I really enjoyed the process and hopefully I'll do it again every year. I'd like to do a bit more pickling and make jams and preserves. It's just that you need to have a few days where you're doing absolutely nothing at all – and that never seems to happen.

We often have a grab-and-share type dinner on a Saturday evening, something like bao buns with some spicy chicken, and I'll do bowls of grated cheese, rice, cucumber and spring onions to go with it. Or it'll be chicken fajitas, chilli – things that you put in the middle of the table and everyone can just help themselves.

While I'm preparing the food, I think back to Saturday evenings with my mum and dad in Islington when I was a kid. I can still smell the chip fat in the kitchen: Mum would be peeling the Maris Pipers while the deep fat fryer was on; she'd wash them, chop them and put them in to fry. Mum's chips were fat, thin, long and short, however they came. They were the best chips. She'd do us each a little steak to go with them and she'd cremate it, but it still tasted good. It's not what I'd choose to eat now, but if my mum were here, I'd say, 'I want the steak how you used to do it, please.' She'd probably chuck a few tomatoes in the frying pan with it.

My dad would not allow tomato ketchup on the table, or mint sauce, mustard or mayonnaise. He'd have Bisto gravy though, which I found really weird. I could have tomato sauce, but I couldn't sit with Dad if I was eating it. My brother David also hates it, and my niece Evie can't stand it, either. 'Get that away from me!' she says. It must be a family thing!

While Mum was cooking, my dad would be doing the books for the paper shop. He didn't open the shop on a Sunday, so this was his time to sit down with his tin and his money bags and tally up the week's takings. I loved seeing all the cash spread out, watching him count the notes and coins.

Back in the day, Dad would get quite emotional about football. If Arsenal had played that day, he'd either be really happy that they'd won or a bit annoyed that they hadn't. The football results would be on, and he'd look and see if he'd won any money on 'the pools', a betting game based on guessing the outcome of football matches. To play the pools, you had to predict score draws in a number of league matches, so it was a bit of lottery really, but the prizes were huge, and millions of people did it every week. Anyone who lived through those times will remember the hypnotic sound of the match scores being read out at around five on a Saturday; it was amazing to listen to, almost meditative, a bit like the shipping forecast. And right up until he passed, if Dad saw you looking happy, he'd say, 'What's happened? Won the pools?'

I can't think of a happier place to be than our house in Islington on a Saturday evening, when the football scores were on, and the fat fryer was heating up.

Saturday is the only day of the week in the English-speaking world that held on to its Latin name – and no one knows why. But there is a theory that maybe it was because Norse had two words for Saturday and neither seemed to suit. The first, *Laugardagr,* translates as 'bathing day' or 'hot water day', an idea that the mud-smeared, animal skin-wearing Ancient Britons weren't overly familiar with; the second, *Sunnunótt,* means 'Sunday Eve' (as in, the day before Sunday), which leaves too much room for confusion.

You can imagine the monk in charge of writing out the new weekday names scratching his head and saying, 'What's a bathing day? FFS, let's just leave it as Saturday, shall we?'

Fun fact: in Finnish, Estonian and modern Maori, the word for Saturday also means 'bathing day'. But in Japanese and Korean, it's 'soil day'.

Telly was a huge part of Saturday evening when I was a kid. It was *Big Break* and *The Generation Game* on the BBC, and then we'd switch over to ITV for *Blind Date* and *Gladiators.* That tradition of watching Saturday night telly together as a family is still something we do in our house today. We're quite old-fashioned like that. Even though you can sit down to eat at half seven these days without missing anything because you've got it all on demand whenever you like, we still like to say, 'What's on telly tonight?'

These days, it's *Michael McIntyre's Big Show, The Masked Singer, Limitless Win* and *The 1% Club.* We used to love *Ant and Dec's Saturday Night Takeaway* as well.

Strictly Come Dancing is great – it's got it all, really. Great costumes, nice music, good routines. I also enjoy watching it because I competed in *Strictly* in 2009, the same year as Ricky Groves, Chris Hollins (who won), Ricky Whittle (runner up), Lynda Bellingham, Jo Wood, Phil Tufnell and Craig Kelly.

Doing *Strictly* was exciting and magical for me. It was also petrifying, because, as with any other performance that scares me, it's live. There's a moment when you're standing at the top of the stairs about to make your entrance, and you know that whatever you do next is going out to the nation and there's nothing you can do about it.

I get dizzy standing at the top of a high staircase at the best of times. Some people like to be up mountains, but I'm not drawn to heights. I needed someone to hold on to, or a rail to steady me, but I had to walk down the stairs on live television with my head held high. I kept thinking I was going to fall. It didn't matter how well I knew the dance I was about to do, as soon as I heard the countdown to the start of the show, my legs would turn to jelly and I'd think, 'I don't know what I'm doing. I've forgotten everything.'

There's nothing like that feeling of going out onto a stage in front of a live audience and millions of people at home, thinking, 'If I muck this up, everybody is going to see it.'

I had a brilliant partner in Vincent Simone, an Italian dancer. Vincent and I had a lovely relationship, like a brother and sister. There was none of this fraternising that can sometimes go on. People get caught up in the throes of passion, but we just got on with the job. Anyway, I have no idea how romance manages to blossom when you've got cameras following you all day and you're going over and over your dance in a PE hall up in Hendon! Maybe it's because of my comical way and because I wasn't an amazing dancer, but for me, the whole thing was vibrant and fun.

We were just laughing all the time, and I loved the sequins and the fake tan.

Bruce Forsyth was presenting the show with Tess Daly back then. Len Goodman was the head judge and Claudia Winkleman was still doing *It Takes Two*. When Bruce was ill with flu one week, Ronnie Corbett stood in for him, so it was a very good year for me, as the Sinatra song goes. I loved Bruce in *The Generation Game* and Ronnie Corbett in *The Two Ronnies*, so it felt like an incredible honour to be working with two of my childhood idols. I'm always attracted to these old characters, but I was also completely awestruck by the two of them. It's a proper thrill to meet someone you've looked up to as a kid. It takes you straight back in time to Saturday nights in front of the telly with Mum and Dad.

Bruce was always saying to the competitors, 'You're my favourite.' It was one of his catchphrases. But when I left, after Vincent and I were voted out in a dance-off with Ricky Whittle and his partner, Bruce was actually teary. He went down on one knee, kissed my hand and said, 'You really are my favourite.' It felt so sincere. We all shed a tear. Vincent was in bits. And Len Goodman gave me a copy of his wonderful autobiography and wrote in it, 'Dearest Natalie, Save the last dance for me, love Len.'

My dad loved my time on *Strictly*. He'd come along and watch in his pinstripe suit. The judges keep their distance until the end of the show, but then they go out with you and have a blast – I seem to remember my dad drinking black tequila shots with Craig Revel Horwood! Or maybe I dreamed that bit, because I've never heard of black tequila since that day. My nieces came along to watch as well, so it was good fun.

Vincent and I got down to the last five, but that wasn't about talent or dancing. I think I stayed in the running because I gave it a go and I'm real, and that's the way I captured the audience. My advice to any celebrity going on *Strictly* would be to be yourself. If you have something to prove and you're not yourself, you won't last long because there really is nowhere to hide.

There have been so many great dancers on *Strictly*. I've loved watching my *EastEnders* friends, of course, and there have been lots of them. Jamie Borthwick, who plays Jay in *EastEnders* and is like another nephew to me, did brilliantly well in 2024, and the best thing about it was that he fell in love with the whole experience and he's still dancing now. Even at my *EastEnders* leaving do, he was trying to get people up to do a rumba. He loved every second of it. I was the same. I really did fall in love with the dancing. Some days I couldn't stop grinning because I was having so much fun. I had the best time of my life.

There's a moment from *Strictly* that gives me goosebumps every time I watch it: Bill Bailey and Oti Mabuse dancing to 'Rapper's Delight'. Bill was one of my favourite contestants ever, and that amazing dance encapsulates the whole programme for me. It's a brilliant show with moments that make your spine tingle. I'm thinking about Chris McCausland dancing to 'You'll Never Walk Alone', and the silent moment that came during Rose Ayling-Ellis's unforgettable dance. It's great that television can still do that. *Strictly* is very inclusive and I think it's a really fantastic programme.

> Saturday is named after Saturn, another multitasking Roman god (like Venus) who wielded power over time, agriculture, growth, abundance, wealth and liberation, among other things. Saturn was believed to have ruled the world during the mythological Golden Age, a time of peace, harmony and plenty.
>
> The wild, carnivalesque ancient Roman festival of Saturnalia was dedicated to Saturn. This was held in December and was characterised by feasting, gambling, revelry, free speech and gift-giving. It started as a one-day holiday, but by the first century CE the party lasted seven days, and in later centuries its traditions were overlaid onto Christmas and New Year.

Three years after *Strictly*, I was invited to take part in two big reality shows. I was suddenly in demand, probably because my turbulent personal life was in the news, and that's often when they swoop. 'We've got a good one here,' they think.

Out of the two shows, I chose Channel 5's *Celebrity Big Brother*. Honestly, I agreed to do it mainly because I had a large tax bill to pay, but I also quite liked the idea of having a break from everything that was going on in my life. My only worry was over how much I was going to miss Eliza, who was only fourteen months old at the time. I knew she was in safe hands with my family, but it was going to be tough being without her.

On 5 January 2012 I made my entrance into the Big Brother house in Borehamwood, which is, oddly, a place that feels like home because it's where the *EastEnders* studios are. I was the first into the house. Instantly, I was given an earpiece and told to do everything Big Brother asked me to do. It was a secret 'icebreaker' task, and it was quite mad: I had to be gratingly nice to a model, fawn embarrassingly over a Hollywood movie star, kiss a young singer on the lips twice and tell him I fancied younger men, speak in an American accent and get everyone to hold hands in a circle while I gave a motivational speech. All on my first day!

I was only in there for sixteen days; I was the fifth to come out. In the days that followed my crazy entrance, I cooked and cleaned and had a bit of a laugh, and I even did a task where I had to walk through treacle. Yes, when anyone ever says to me that something is 'like walking through treacle', I say, 'Ah, have you ever done that? I've actually done it.' It's an apt phrase because it's really not easy to walk through treacle. It's very difficult, in fact.

When I was voted out of the *Celebrity Big Brother* house, it was all a big shock horror among the other contestants, but I was thrilled because it meant I could get back to Eliza. It was quite nice to have some time away from the outside world, but I had missed her dearly.

During my time in the house, I made great friends with the actress and presenter Denise Welch, who was brilliant and very kind to me. Some of the other people were a bit bonkers, though. 'What is all this that's going on around me?' I kept thinking.

It felt very Andy Millman from *Extras* – in the Christmas special, the last-ever episode, he does *Celebrity Big Brother* because he thinks it's going to be great and meets all these really sad people who want to be famous. It was poignant then, and, I think, more poignant than ever in today's world.

That desperation for fame is a bit cringeworthy to me. I know some people would love to be as well known as I am and I can't say I hate being famous, but I think if it ebbed away naturally, I wouldn't try to rekindle it.

Hopefully, I use it in a positive way, because I'm not fame-hungry. And there's part of it that's brilliant. Without it, I wouldn't have the opportunities that arise as a result of it – like getting to write this book! – and I know it and appreciate those things. But I see it as a career – it's my job. My brother David is a bank manager, my other brother Tony is a builder and I'm an actress and a celebrity. I don't see mine as better than any other job; it just so happens that this is the job I have.

The compliments that come my way are lovely, but it's the same as Tony being complimented for doing a brilliant bathroom. That said, you do get a lot of smoke blowing up your bottom in this world. People think it must be quite hard sometimes to navigate through it, but I think I've got a sixth sense of knowing if someone's 'real' or not.

Some of the most insecure people are actors and actresses,

but if you are thin-skinned in this industry, you have a much harder time of it, especially if you are catapulted into fame from a young age, as I was. It can go one way or the other – I think a lot of it probably comes down to your background and the family support you've been given. I can recognise that I've been very fortunate throughout my life. Having a job from a young age means I've never had to think about what I want to be or want to do – I just carried on doing the job I began doing at ten years old! I've never had to go for loads of job interviews or auditions and so haven't had a lot of rejection in my life. I've been lucky in that regard – and I always loved my work too much to go off the rails like some child actors do. I never wanted to let anybody down.

In fact, I think if you asked any of my friends or family, I'm sure they'd tell you I'm the same as I've always been. I don't know why that is, honestly. I think it's just me; it's in my genetic make-up to be down to earth and grounded, and all these years in the public eye really haven't changed that.

You can't be too cynical in life. You should be able to be proud of your achievements and accept a compliment in any walk of life. I think it's becoming more socially acceptable now, especially for women, to be openly proud of themselves and say, 'I'm great, and I'm doing this.'

Even so, you can't help but be conscious of the fact that people might be thinking, 'Look at her! She's flash. She's got an ego,' or even, 'Who does she think she is with her nose stuck up in the air?'

Ever since I did *Celebrity Big Brother*, people have asked

me if I would consider doing ITV's *I'm a Celebrity . . .Get Me Out of Here!* I always say the same thing: never say never!

I'm a real fan of the show – always have been. I love Ant and Dec, and we enjoy watching the show as a family. But I feel like I would have to be really brave to go into the jungle – brave in a different way from performing on *Strictly* or doing silly tasks in the Big Brother house. I am such a scaredy-cat that I have a feeling I would be one of those annoying people who gets picked for all the trials and challenges, and the idea of that isn't very appealing to me. There's another reason, as well: I talk honestly and openly – I just can't help myself – and maybe that isn't such a good idea when millions of people are watching you.

Would celebrities do the show if they didn't need the money? I'm not sure. I think some people do it for profile reasons. If they're just starting out in the game and they think they'll raise their profile, I understand it. Otherwise, unless you've got a hefty tax bill or you're not really earning money, I'm not sure why you'd go into the jungle.

Lovely Jacqueline Jossa, a good friend of mine, was Queen of the Jungle in 2019, and she did brilliantly well out of it. She went in there and it really changed her career. For Coleen Rooney in 2024, it was a fantastic way to come out and demonstrate what a wonderful woman she is, and show that she loves Wayne and sticks by him. She came across as a solid, caring human being who stands by her morals and what she believes in.

I'd say that my all-time fave contestant was Dean Gaffney

though. He played my brother Robbie in *EastEnders*, and I adore him. He's a great guy and a gentleman, always on time for work. It was very, very funny when Dean went into the jungle, and I really enjoyed watching him on the sixth series of *I'm a Celebrity* . . . I still watch his Bushtucker Trials on YouTube sometimes. He's so over-the-top scared – it's hilarious.

Maybe one day in the future, I will be brave and do it, but, at this point in time, I think I'm probably okay.

All these types of shows are scary. Fifteen years after I plucked up the courage to go out every week and dance live on *Strictly*, I experienced a similar feeling of terror in the lead up to another live performing show, *The Masked Singer*, on ITV. For anyone who hasn't watched it, I'll quickly explain. It's a singing competition based on a Korean format, where the performers hide their identity by wearing completely mad costumes and masks, while singing in front of a live audience and a panel of judges. The judges rate the performances and try to guess the identities of the competitors, and there's also a public vote. It's a process of elimination, and one contestant leaves the show every week.

Taking part in *The Masked Singer* was almost as terrifying as doing *Strictly*, but not quite. It was filmed live, but it wasn't broadcast live, so if I'd fallen over, I might have been given the chance to do another take, which isn't a possibility on *Strictly*.

The whole thing came about by chance – it really was a case of being in the right place at the right time. I went to an awards ceremony and as I was coming out of the loo,

I saw the lovely Liz Holmwood, a talent producer, chatting away with the comedian Katherine Ryan in a corridor. I've known Liz a long, long time and think she's wonderful and funny, so I went up and gave her a hug.

'I was just talking to Katherine about her experience on *The Masked Singer* last year,' she said. 'It's such a shame you can't do it.'

'When do you film it?' I asked.

When she told me the dates, I thought, 'Wait a minute!'

'We need to have a chat, because I've got a break from *EastEnders* then,' I told Liz.

When we talked again, we realised that the filming schedule for *The Masked Singer* fitted perfectly with a four-month period where I had taken unpaid leave from *EastEnders* to work on a Channel 4 consumer affairs documentary, *What's The Big Deal?* It was also when I was planning to really focus on my podcast, which started broadcasting in April 2024. So, although I was already going to be busy over the summer and autumn, it was ridiculously good timing. When they asked me to do it, I happily accepted.

After I'd signed up, I had a meeting with the costume designers to go through some of the ideas and concepts for my character. *The Masked Singer* wardrobe department is amazing – it really does have to be seen to be believed – and we went through some really wacky costumes before this massive bush costume came up. It was covered in leaves, roses and twigs, and had great big eyes. 'That's it, I have to be Bush,' I thought. 'It's so camp and funny; it's hilarious.

Just imagine: "Here comes the bush!" "Has she trimmed her bush?"'

I've got a strong LGBTQ+ following because of Sonia and her place in Nineties pop culture. Sonia, in her brides-maid's dress, with her trumpet in her hand, went from being a Nineties icon to finding a place in Hun culture when Gareth Howells set up Hunsnet. There's a really lovely, warm audience of people that love Sonia. I knew they would all absolutely roar with laughter at this costume, and they did. They loved the fact that I was a big bush.

'You're our comic turn this year,' one of the producers told me.

'I'm not a comedian,' I said, but it was lovely to be seen in that way.

It was such a fun job. For about six or seven weeks, I was secretly going off for singing lessons once a week; I was picking the songs and learning them with the help of some brilliant singing teachers. You get a nice cup of coffee as well, so all in all, it was a really lovely thing to do, and no one in the family had a clue, apart from Marc. That was another fun part – keeping quiet about what I'm up to work-wise is fairly standard, but this time I was really looking forward to seeing everyone's reaction when they found out I was Bush, especially my girls – I thought it would be really fun if I could get them to watch it like any other TV show, no idea that it was their mum up there.

At the start of my first lesson, I was told off by one of the teachers for saying that I'm not a singer. 'Everyone can sing,' he said. 'It's all about breathing and being aware of your muscles and how you use them.'

So, okay, I'm not a *trained* singer, and I didn't rate my singing potential much, either.

'You've come a really long way from when you first walked into this space,' the teachers told me in my final lesson.

It was nice of them to say so, but I was incredibly nervous about my ability to sing onstage. My lips went dry as a stress response and I was constantly having to plaster them in Vaseline so that they didn't crack or stick to my teeth. We had this joke in the studio about it, because I kept asking the lovely assistants, 'Have you got the pot of Vaseline? You have got it, haven't you?' and they would follow me round with it all the time we were filming.

It was terrifying coming out on stage the first week. You could hear my voice shaking in my performance. I was petrified, because, whatever my teachers said, I really am not a singer. It was a little better the second week, and I am a big believer in feeling the fear and doing it anyway, but the whole thing was a huge challenge.

I thought I'd be knocked out quickly. The first week, I was in the bottom two, voted by the public, but the panel saved me, and then I stayed in the running right up until the final. I didn't have a clue who else was performing. I'd come off stage and a producer would say, 'You won't believe who's been knocked out tonight,' or 'You'll never believe who you were just standing next to.' It wasn't until it was broadcast in early 2025 that I watched it all unfold, and only then did

I discover that the other contestants included Grayson Perry, Macy Gray, Gregory Porter, Prue Leith, Andrea Corr, Kate Garraway, Mel Giedroyc and Samantha Barks, who won it.

Joanie had no idea I was Bush, bless her. It was the funniest thing, because when we watched it at home, I could see that she was naturally drawn to the Bush character without having any idea that it was me. Neither of the girls had any idea until the penultimate week, and then it was only because Eliza kept getting text messages from friends and comments from teachers at school that they began to twig. 'Is your mum on *The Masked Singer*?'

Loads of people were suspicious by my final week – I think my voice is very distinctive. But that's the fun of it: no one really knows until the mask comes off. It's a brilliant secret to keep.

On the week of my final appearance, I had some of the family over for a takeaway. By this point, a lot of them were saying, 'This is you. This is why you've got us over.'

'But you always come over! It's a normal thing for you to come over,' I said, a little bit tongue-in-cheek.

The moment when the mask came off was brilliant. Everyone was screaming and leaping around the living room when they realised it was me. Joanie was really excited. Eliza, being a teen, had mixed feelings. 'I'm so embarrassed,' she wailed.

The Masked Singer is the weirdest thing I've ever done and definitely one of the scariest. I was massively stepping out of my comfort zone and I feel really proud that I did it. Learning a new skill was a fantastic confidence boost too. If I ever do a pantomime in the future, or any other part that requires singing, I feel like maybe I could belt out a tune now, with a little bit of help. It's another string to your bow, and that's always a good thing to have as you go through life.

I had a lot of positive comments after it came out; I think people were quite impressed because they could tell it wasn't an easy thing to do. It felt like a great way to kick off the year – the first of many different things.

I learned a big lesson, though, from those months spent running around filming *What's the Big Deal?* and *The Masked Singer*. I ended up working myself to death because all these brilliant opportunities had arisen and I only had a small window to squeeze them into. One day I'd be filming for the documentary, the next day I'd rush off to *The Masked Singer* and then it would be straight back into the documentary. On top of all that, I was also doing my first season of podcast shows.

That period was supposed to be a little break for me, but I barely had a weekend off and so the break didn't happen. These days, I'm much stricter with myself. I've left *EastEnders*, which means that there isn't a tight window that I have fit everything into, so when I'm offered a project and my diary is full, I can say, 'I'd love to do that next year,' or, 'Can we have a look at that in a few months' time?'

I'm also thrilled because the podcast is doing really well, so I don't need to say yes to everything. As long as it continues that way, anything else is a bonus. I don't need to be running around so much, which means I can focus more on the projects that I really want to do.

It's taken a few years to get here, but I finally have more autonomy.

*

Sleep is so important but getting eight hours' sleep isn't always possible. Life is just too busy. Once the kids are in bed, I want some 'me' time, and I can feel a bit robbed if I don't get to have it. It's just nice to be able to relax and have that time with Marc when you're not answering questions; when it's not 'Mum, Mum, Mum . . .'

There are nights, though, when I say, 'Come on, let's go to bed early.' We always go to bed at the same time; although Marc might be quite contented to stay sat on the sofa, he'll still say, 'Okay, I'll be up in a minute.'

Once I'm in bed, I'm a bit like a child. 'Marc, are you coming?' Honestly, it's probably not fair on him because I'll call out, 'Come on, come to bed. Turn the lights off.' We don't get into bed and immediately turn our lights off, though. We're terrible for our phones in bed, which needs to stop; we've been having lots of conversations about that. Saying that, I'm not scrolling on the phone; I'm doing the things that need doing, like looking at fixtures for our bathroom refit or checking my emails, or else I'm looking at my business WhatsApp for the pod to see if there are any interesting messages or getting back to fans who have messaged me on

Instagram. I like to connect with people, and I think it's good for them to know there's a possibility that I will answer them. I'm not some unreachable person. I'm not untouchable.

Depending on what I've posted that day, sometimes I can't keep up with it all, but it's still nice to do a little casino whizz through the messages and write a reply or two, to spin the roulette wheel and see what you come up with. It means that someone will get an answer that day, which I think is quite nice.

Chapter Nine

Sunday

Sunday is one of my favourite days of the week because it's a day with the family. I know the kids will be around, and I'll be able to have a lay-in.

I do love a lay-in. It makes me yawn just saying it! I love my bed and I don't feel guilty about it. Being quite old-fashioned, I also like a newspaper. Maybe it's because it reminds me of Dad and the newsagents. Thinking about it now though, I used to love having a newspaper on a Sunday, but I've actually not bought a paper in . . . I can't even tell you how long. I think I might start that again and get the *Observer* or *The Sunday Times*. It's nice to sit in bed and go through all of the different supplements, and it's not the same reading it on your phone or an iPad, is it?

As I say to Marc, that's one of the reasons I love going away with him to a hotel for a couple of nights. The sex is good, but the paper . . . !

One of our best weekends was spent in a hotel in Killarney in Ireland. It was so idyllic. We had a gorgeous room with a hot tub on the balcony. In the evenings, we went out to pubs and drank pints of Guinness. While we were there,

I promised myself that we'd do it again soon, and we will. It's just that life gets in the way – other things take over and opportunities arise.

When I'm working really hard and wishing I could be on holiday, I like to remind myself: 'I'm building all of this for more of that.' Marc and I both say it to each other: 'We're building, building, building.'

Joanie has been getting up and going downstairs on her own since she was about five. She's an independent little thing: she wakes up, comes in, gives us a kiss, then goes down and puts the telly on while I'll stay in bed for another couple of hours. Whether people think it's right, wrong or indifferent, she's quite content. She'll watch a bit of telly, peel a banana, and then eventually, she'll come up and say, 'Mum, I'm actually hungry and bored now.' That's my cue to get up.

In recent weeks though, Joanie has taken to putting the telly on really loudly in the morning. You've never heard anything like it! It's ridiculous, and I'm sure she does it on purpose to get us all up bright and early with her.

Now she's older, Eliza likes a lay-in these days, which I think is extremely important for kids, especially teenagers. Sleep is such an integral part of forming the adolescent brain. I've never been one to wake her up when she's sleeping. I'll leave her be, shut the door, keep it dark, and tell Joanie not to go disturbing her. It doesn't bother me if Eliza doesn't rise until half eleven or twelve; I think it's really healthy, and she obviously needs the extra sleep.

I usually have a little look at my private Instagram first thing on a Sunday morning. It's nice to see if anyone's messaged. The business WhatsApp for my podcast is on my phone, and so I'll click onto that next. I've got different groups and subjects for the different podcasts I do, so I'll be shuffling the voicenotes and messages into groups. Messages are constantly coming through, so it's a bit of a never-ending job; even doing five minutes of it here and there helps me keep on top of it. If I left it and suddenly had three hundred messages to look at, I think it could become overwhelming.

Next, I'll go down to the kitchen, have a cup of tea and either start on the roast or whizz along to my lovely local farm shop to pick up some of the last bits and pieces. I don't need inspiration in the kitchen on a Sunday – it's got to be a roast. Mine is always a winner with the kids, so nine times out of ten that's what I'll make.

If all the food is in, I'll be peeling potatoes, prepping the veg and getting my Yorkshire pudding mix made, so that I'm ready and sorted for later in the day. I love making my own cauliflower cheese, too. I usually use a very lovely Cornish Cruncher, a strong cheddar from M&S, and I put in a lot of cheese and butter. I don't worry about using lots of butter because you need it to make a good roast; I also use a ton of olive oil for my roast potatoes, as the girls like them really crunchy.

I love roast potatoes with garlic and rosemary, but the girls prefer a plain roast dinner. I think it stems back to when my dad was living with us, because he hated garlic and he hated herbs, so I always cooked a very plain roast using salt as my only seasoning and it's what the girls are used to.

Cooking a roast is all about timing, and I'm very good with timing! First things first, weigh your meat. Look up how long it's going to take and work backwards from that number. If you're cooking a cut of beef that takes ninety minutes, for instance, then you can plan when everything else goes in so that it's all ready at the same time. People say a roast is such a faff, but it's easy really – you just have to get your timings right.

I like to have everything prepared before I put the oven on. So, after my potatoes are peeled, boiled and drained, I fluff them and they're ready to go. After the carrots and parsnips are peeled, I parboil them for a little while, but not for so long that it takes the goodness out. My peas and broccoli are in their saucepans. The batter for my Yorkshire puddings is mixed. Everything's ready to go.

The meat should be in a dish, seasoned, resting outside the fridge for a good hour and a half to two hours, before you cook it. The oven goes on, very, very hot, and the meat goes in. You shouldn't need longer than an hour to do your potatoes, parsnips, carrots and other vegetables. The cauliflower cheese is already made.

When the meat comes out of the oven, it rests for ten or fifteen minutes, and that's when my Yorkshire puddings go in. They need to cook on a really high heat, so I make sure that my potatoes also need that high heat to crisp them up and I make them as crunchy as time allows.

It's a good old plain roast, and I do pretty much the same thing every time, mainly for the children. I might change things up a bit if we have guests coming over, but actually, I like the simplicity of how a plain roast comes together.

Sometimes, I'll put the meat in, and then we'll stroll over to the pub as a family, the four of us, and catch up with people from the village. Going to the pub gives us a chance to see how the neighbours are, have a little chat. An hour quickly goes by, and I'll have my eye on the clock because I'm timing the meat. Anyway, an hour is enough for the girls to be in the pub. I don't like taking them for longer than that. You sometimes see children sat on iPads or phones in pubs and there's something about it that I find quite sad. Yes, the parents might be having a nice time, but is a pub really the best place for a child? There are lots more fun places for kids to be. An hour is enough for Joanie, if she has a lemonade and a packet of crisps to keep her going. It's a nice amount of time, and then we'll head home and have dinner.

When I was a kid, the Sunday roast was sacred, and my mum would always do it for 2 p.m. I remember playing Rummy, Snap! and Tiddlywinks with Daddy, and watching *The Smurfs* while Mummy made Sunday lunch. It would always be a very calm, slow day, and I've definitely taken that on board. I enjoy a relaxed day where the girls are doing homework, and I have a little potter with the radio on and cook the roast. Following in Mum's footsteps, I used to be really strict and want to eat at two-ish as well, but now we might pop over to the pub at four, and we'll eat any time between four and six o'clock. Now that Joanie's getting older, we can be a bit more flexible. She's not exhausted by a quarter to seven and you're not panicking that she's falling asleep into her dinner. She goes to bed at eight-ish now, so it all works out pretty well.

Sunday is also the day to get together with the wider family. If it's my nieces and nephew on the Cassidy side of the family, you're probably looking at fourteen or fifteen of us, and I'll cook a big roast for everyone. It's lovely when they're all here – the adults are having a nice time, and the kids are all playing.

If the family come round in the summer, I'll do two or three roast chickens, a few big bowls of different salads and chuck a load of wedges in the oven.

'Nat, will you do the pear and walnut salad for me?' my niece Maria will ask.

It is yummy – I mix together chicory leaves, blue cheese, chopped walnuts, pear slices and truffle honey. You can serve it in individual portions, with everything piled on a chicory leaf, or mixed up in a big salad. If it's not the pear and walnut salad it'll be, 'I really fancy some beetroot.'

So off I'll go and find beetroot. The other day, I bought rainbow beetroots, the colourful ones, which I love. I peeled them all, chucked a load of sea salt on them, roasted them, sliced them thinly and laid them out on a bed of the M&S Collection summer shoots salad. I chucked some little lumps of goat cheese all over it, drizzled olive oil on top and sprinkled salt over it. Maria loved it. Seal of approval!

Some people have tomato ketchup with their roast dinner, or they have mayonnaise on their roast potatoes. Now, if I'm having a breaded piece of chicken with a salad and potatoes, I'll have mayonnaise – and that's come with age, because we didn't have it in the house when I was young, so I wouldn't have known whether I liked it or not. But mayonnaise with gravy? I don't think so.

Then again, you can have English mustard or horseradish with your beef; you can have apple sauce with your pork, and mint sauce with your lamb. So, the roast dinner condiments are allowed in my house, but I will not have a bottle of ketchup on my table on a Sunday. Absolutely not happening.

I'm not a pudding person, and that means we're not really a pudding family. It's selfish of me but I haven't got a sweet tooth, and pudding really does seem to go unnoticed. I might do strawberries and cream in the summer, and if people are coming, they'll bring a dessert – some profiteroles or a cheesecake, but I find it never seems to get eaten because everyone's far too full up. If I do have a pudding, I like a lemon posset, or panna cotta. Something with a little sharpness. I'd rather have a bowl of nice chocolates on the table. I think a little sweet after a meal is enough.

When I was a kid, I spent those few hours after Sunday dinner up in my bedroom, recording and writing down the Top 40 countdown as it was announced on Radio 1. I'd wait to find out the number one, and then it was back downstairs again, sometime between six and seven, for a crumpet. I'd maybe have a shower, get my stuff ready for school and sit and watch the *Antiques Roadshow* with a growing sense of dread, thinking 'Oh God, I've got school tomorrow, I haven't done all my homework.'

I don't have that dread that I used to have on Sunday evening as a kid, and I haven't ever really experienced that sense of foreboding as an adult, because I've always loved what I do. I know how lucky I am. There are lots of people who dread the week starting again and having to go back to work.

> After dinner, we'll usually get a board game or a pack of cards out and play something around the table: Deal or No Deal is a bit of a favourite at the moment; it's simple and fun. Happy Families is another.
>
> Board games have been a huge part of my life from a very young age. Scrabble was the first and then obviously the classic, Monopoly, which I used to play with my nieces. The Game of Life was a really good game where you travel along a pathway to retirement, choosing a career path or a family path as you go. There was Go for Broke, where you are chasing a fortune of millions; Pazazz, a cards, numbers and dice game, was also brilliant. I've still got it, in fact. I've got two cupboards filled with board games, so I am a bit of board game hoarder!
>
> We haven't grown out of games as we've grown up. During Covid, Maria did a quiz every Saturday night. It would last three and a half hours, at least. There would be twenty-five people on Zoom and we'd have a drink, so

it felt like we were all together. On games nights, we play Scattergories, where each player writes a list of answers on a certain theme, and they have to begin with the same letter. Other favourites are Articulate and Guess Who?

I am the least competitive person when it comes to board games. I just want to play a game and enjoy it, but no one wants to be on my team because I don't care if I win or not. I'd actually rather see someone else win than win myself. It's like giving presents – I prefer to watch people open presents than open them myself.

Roast beef on a Sunday was my mum's signature dish. I do roast beef as well, and roast chicken, but I'm not a massive fan of lamb. I love pork, but pork doesn't love me. I'll still eat it though – I'm a bit of a glutton like that. I really shouldn't eat seafood as my body can't tolerate it – I couldn't sit and eat a lobster because I would be ill with a bad tummy, and yet I will still have a bit of lobster all the same. Or I'll think, 'Stuff it, I'm having crab chilli linguine,' even when I know it'll kill me the next day. I shouldn't eat cheese for the same reason – I'm just a bit intolerant – but I ignore it all really; I just think life's too short to stop eating things I like, so I suffer the consequences.

We really love food in our house, and fortunately, Marc is a great cook. He hasn't got the confidence to just chuck stuff together, but he's happy and away once he gets the hang of a recipe. His portfolio is growing. He makes curry, chilli, carbonara, shepherd's pie, and he's very good at eggs. Poached eggs, scrambled eggs and omelettes; he's just annoyingly good at eggs.

I really like taking inspiration for my cooking from restaurants. I'll often go out and see and taste things, and then try and reproduce them at home. One weekend, I wanted to do something really special, and so Marc and I did some monkfish fillets with celeriac velouté. I found the recipe in one of my many cookbooks. I've got hundreds and hundreds of cookbooks and I love them – I love books in general, but especially cookbooks! It was a complicated recipe – totally *MasterChef* – and it took forever.

The problem with dishes like that is that you spend all this time making it, and then you stuff it down within about ten minutes. Unfortunately, the velouté didn't turn out amazingly. The texture came out quite well and it looked like a foam, which was the aim, so that was quite good. The whole thing needed to be seasoned properly, so it was a bit of a disappointment. I had better results when I made a Heston Blumenthal crab lasagna once. But that took forever, as well.

When you make something at home like that foam velouté, or a crisped spinach leaf, it really makes you realise how long these elements take to make. It does make you think differently about what you're paying for when you go to an expensive restaurant. A tasting menu with a wine pairing can cost a lot of money, but the food you're having is a work of art. There are probably nine elements in one tiny dish. That little gel blob on your plate has been prepared by three different people. The skill and time that has gone into every single part of it is worth every penny because you're never going to be able to recreate something like that at home. You haven't got the equipment, you haven't got the temperatures, and you probably don't have the know-how.

What I like about a tasting menu is that the whole thing feels like an amazing, theatrical experience. It's not only about the good food; it's the theatre when you go in. As soon as you walk into the restaurant, they're starting a performance. The waiting staff are a fount of knowledge, and you get the chance to chat to the chefs about all the different elements of the dishes. They can tell you where they've sourced all the ingredients; everything is fresh.

There's a restaurant in Notting Hill, The Ledbury, where every dish they do is outstandingly delicious. I had a mushroom there once that tasted like a fillet steak. You poured an Earl Grey tea over it, which you wouldn't think would work, but it was incredible. I've never tasted anything like it.

I also really love the trickery of a tasting menu. You're served something and you think, 'Is it pudding?' And it's not. It's beef dripping with smoked trout. The bread is just amazing, too. Flavours you wouldn't imagine.

I've had a few tasting menus in London, in restaurants and hotels. They've all been good, and some are more reasonably priced than others. Tom Sellers' Restaurant Story has a really lovely tasting menu with a playlist to go with it. When we're out of London, in Cornwall or somewhere else by the coast, we always try and go to a good restaurant as a treat. Rick Stein's seafood restaurant in Padstow is amazing!

I love food and cooking so much that I was thrilled to be asked to take part in *Cooking with the Stars* for ITV, because I knew how much I would learn. *Cooking with the Stars* is a really lovely show presented by Emma Willis and Tom Allen; it has a touch of *MasterChef*, but it's less demanding. With *MasterChef*, you need the time to put your heart and soul into it and really think about everything, whereas this is a little bit easier and has more entertainment value, in my opinion. The way it works is this: each contestant is paired off with a chef who teaches them how to cook certain dishes. Back in the studio, you have to recreate those dishes in front of the mentor chefs, who decide who will be advancing into the next round and who will be in a cook-off between the bottom two celebs.

I can honestly say I think it's the best job I have ever done. I have such a passion for restaurants and food that it was a treat to be surrounded by these amazing chefs. Facing the pressure of having to cook every day was intense. It was such a rollercoaster: you go from elation to stress to nerves to panic to joy. The amazement you feel when you have actually created and finished a dish, and then to stand in front of the mentor chefs as they taste and judge your cooking, is something else.

The vegetarian dishes I learned you just would not believe, including Chole Masala, which is chickpea curry, and a lentil dal that just tasted amazing. I did a lot of Indian-inspired cooking, including some really lovely fried chicken and waffles with an Indian twist. But I also made a mushroom fideuà, which is a Spanish pasta dish. You fry off the pasta before boiling it, so that it's a golden-brown colour, and then when you boil it, it ends up with an earthy, nutty flavour. It was a bit like the mushroom I had at The Ledbury, in that it tasted really meaty without having any meat in it. It was so exciting to be experimenting with flavours and discovering new dishes.

I was told on the show that you either have a good palate or you don't, in terms of being able to identify subtle differences in taste. Knowing when there's enough depth of flavour or not can't really be learned; it's just there in our tastebuds, our sense of smell and our brain signals.

I met so many interesting people over the course of filming, and it's what I love about getting to work on different jobs – it opens you up to conversations you'd never usually have. Each night after filming, we got the chance to socialise with the chefs, and it was so interesting to hear them talking. I just sat there listening, taking in every word. It was fascinating to hear Jack Stein talk about his father, Rick, and all the stuff he does in Cornwall, because obviously I love Cornwall.

For my final dish, I elevated what I love to do on a Sunday and did a special kind of roast, a pork chop with a deep fried sausage bonbon, crispy new potatoes, roasted carrots glazed with clementine orange and apple juice, and apple puree made from scratch. There was a lot of work, but it went down well and I then went on to win the competition. It just goes to show: you can't beat a Sunday roast!

The Sunday roast originated in Yorkshire, but is eaten all over the world, especially – but not exclusively – in countries where English is spoken. In some places, they replace their Yorkshire puddings with rice and gravy, which doesn't sound quite right to me, and in South Africa, instead of having a Yorkshire pudding, they go totally off-piste and serve up maize porridge with tomato gravy. I suppose roast dinners are like people and languages – they evolve.

The French call the Brits 'rosbifs' but often eat a rotisserie chicken with potatoes and veg on a Sunday, which isn't a million miles away from a roast chicken dinner, n'est-ce pas? In China, they might have Peking duck, which is roasted duck served with pancakes, cucumber and hoisin sauce. Or dim sum, delicious little steamed or fried dishes: spiced dumplings, buns, rice balls, noodle rolls, all with unique flavours.

On a Sunday in South American countries like Chile and Argentina, it's 'asado', a fancy meat barbecue, because they've got the weather, haven't they? In Brazil, it's either a barbecue or feijoada, a slow-cooked meat and black bean stew extravaganza.

In Spain, it's paella, and I really do love a paella. To make it properly, you need a wide, flat paellera dish to cook it with, so that you slightly burn the rice on the bottom. You also need real saffron, which is an expensive spice, but you only need a few strands to turn the rice yellow and give it its unique fragrance. (You can also cheat and use a bit of turmeric when no one is looking, shhh.)

On Sundays in winter, the Russians ward off the cold weather with a hearty soup like borscht followed by meat and potatoes. The Indians, not having that problem with cold weather so much, favour biryani, a fragrant rice dish made with spices, meat and veg. In Nigeria, it's jollof rice, made with onions, chillis, spices, tomatoes and meat or fish, served with a stew or a soup.

In another life, I'd love to be a travelling food writer, sampling scrumptious dishes all over the world. It makes me hungry just thinking about it.

Sunday is not a very exciting day, and that's what is nice about it, I think. Until the Sunday trading restrictions were lifted in 1994, the idea of Sunday shopping as a leisure activity was unheard of, and the majority of people didn't have to go to work. It was a family-and-friends day, when you had a roast at home, went to visit to relatives or got in the car for a Sunday drive.

When life went at a slower pace, Sunday had a reputation for being a boring day when there was nothing to do. Nowadays, I can't imagine being bored because there's so much to do all the time.

Sunday is named after Sunna, or Sol, the Norse goddess who drives the Sun across the sky in a chariot pulled by two horses, Árvakr (meaning 'early awake') and Alsviðr ('very swift'). According to mythology, Sol is Mani, the moon god's, sister. She is being chased across the sky by a hungry wolf named Sköll, who will eventually devour her at Ragnorok, when the world ends.

According to today's scientists, what will actually happen, several billion years from now, is that the Sun's core will heat up and turn it into a red giant (a bit too hot for Earth-dwellers) before it becomes a dense cooling star known as a white dwarf (remaining hot for trillions of years) and then a black dwarf (not much heat or energy). Different story, same outcome: freezing cold darkness.

The Greek word for the sun is 'helios'. The scientific study of the Sun is called 'heliology'. And 'heliac' is a rare adjective in the English language that means 'relating to the sun'. So, you could say, 'It's a heliacal day today,' and, 'I like people who have heliacal personalities.' Only, it just doesn't sound as good as 'sunny', does it?

Chapter Ten

Christmas Day

I start thinking about Christmas even before Halloween and Bonfire Night are over. I'm itching by then for the big day, and honestly, I can't wait to get them out of the way so that I can get on with the best holiday of the year.

At the beginning of October, I'm thinking, 'Right, what are we going to do this year, then?' I start opening all my Christmas books and looking at ideas and recipes. I just get very excited. In case you haven't guessed already, Christmas is my absolute favourite time of year.

It's no coincidence that Christmas Day is held very close to the winter solstice, the shortest day of the year, when the sun is at its lowest in the sky and because of the tilt in the earth's axis, the northern hemisphere is furthest away from it.

In Roman times, when the calendars weren't totally accurate, they held a festival celebrating the birthday of the sun on 25 December. This was exactly nine months after the spring equinox, which by their calculations was 25 March (and later decided to be the date of Jesus's conception). It was also just after the festival of Saturnalia, where people feasted, gambled and cavorted for days on end. The whole lot got mixed and merged in the fourth century, when Christianity became the official religion of the Roman Empire. Yay! 'Eat, drink and be merry, for tomorrow we die,' as it sort of says in the Bible. In fact, it's the combination of two biblical passages, and isn't meant to mean what it is commonly taken to mean, lol.

I usually make my Christmas puddings and mincemeat in October. I make mini-Christmas puddings and give them out: one to a neighbour, another to a friend. I've given them to work friends, as well; I've taken them a jar of mincemeat or a little pud. Last year, I didn't get to do it because I didn't have any time, and I was devastated. If I have the time, though, I think it's really special to give out something you've made yourself. It's just a really nice way of showing someone you've thought of them, and taken a bit of time over something.

I use Delia's recipe for my mincemeat and puddings. I don't think you can beat *Delia Smith's Christmas* book for puds. The first stage of the pudding is easy. You soak all your fruit the night before; you chuck it in a huge bowl with suet, breadcrumbs, spices, sugar, a chopped apple and orange and lemon zest, pour a load of booze over it and leave it overnight. Delia recommends using brandy, barley wine and a good stout. The following day, you steam it for eight hours, which doesn't require a lot of effort, though you do have to keep an eye on it, obviously.

The mincemeat isn't difficult, either. You combine all the ingredients and leave it overnight, but don't add the brandy until after you've cooked it. Once you've made your own mincemeat, you realise that how huge the difference is between homemade and shop-bought. You almost can't compare them, and it's hard to go back to the jarred stuff once you've made your own.

> In medieval times, mince pies were known as 'Christmas pies', 'shrid pies' and 'crib cakes' and made with mutton and beef, or pork, rabbit or game – along with fruit and spices. Sometimes they were symbolically shaped like a manger, with the spices said to represent the gifts of the Three Wise Men of the Nativity, and the lamb representing the shepherds.
>
> Historical records show that Henry V had a big mince pie at his coronation in 1413, and there is a sixteenth-century record of a mince pie so enormous that it contained the meat of a whole leg of mutton, among other ingredients. In the north of England, they stacked theirs with goose or beef tongue.
>
> In the eighteenth century, there was a shift towards sweeter, meatless mince pies and the Victorians shrank them to bring them even closer to the mince pie as we know it. Eventually, along came Mr Kipling and its mammoth twenty-acre factory in Barnsley that produces hundreds of mince pies every minute . . .

When I'm making mince pies, I buy rather than make my pastry, unlike my mum. She always made hers from scratch and I remember her running her hands under the cold tap while she was making it. 'You must have cold hands, a cold bowl and cold utensils whilst making pastry,' she'd tell me.

I buy mine purely because that's what a lot of chefs suggest: 'Just buy ready-rolled.' Even Mary Berry says it. I'm not saying that I wouldn't make pastry if I had the time, but for now, I buy it in packets – puff and shortcrust – and that way, it's not quite as heartbreaking if Joanie decides she wants to roll it up and play with it!

Marc made a lovely Christmas cake last year. Out of the two of us, he is the baker. Marc loves making banana muffins, and he does a great marmalade cake. I'm not massive on baking because I haven't got a sweet tooth. I'd love to learn, but with time being precious, I cook what I enjoy eating, and that's savoury stuff. We go with our own tastes, don't we? Eliza was on *Junior Bake Off* and used to like making cookies, but she's not that interested in it now. She's far too busy chatting to her friends, which is fair enough. I'm sure it'll come back to her.

By October, I'm also thinking about the table for Christmas. Am I going to buy any new decorations? Who's coming? Where am I placing everybody? Marc's family are a bit more laid back about plans than I am, so when I send out a quick WhatsApp in September or October, saying, *What's everyone thinking about Christmas?* they'll come back with, *No, Nat, please don't mention Christmas! Let's not talk about it yet.*

I like to know well in advance what I'm doing on Christmas

Day, Boxing Day, and the day after. I like to know who is going to be where and when.

'Any thoughts? Where's everyone going? Is everybody happy?' I need to know. I probably completely overthink it, and people will be absolutely fine wherever they are, but I like to feel I'm doing the right thing. I want to see everyone and make sure no one's offended. Christmas can be a hard time for people, can't it? Family politics, who's coming around, who isn't, who's going where.

Families grow. Families get bigger. My niece, Evie May, and James, my nephew, have partners now, so they might be with their partners' families instead of with us for Boxing Day and that's totally fine. People have elderly parents, and they don't want to leave them on their own. Maria and Ellia have their own babies and children now. So, it's not just your family to plan for anymore, is it? There are a lot of in-laws, and people have to visit everyone, so there's quite a lot to factor in. I'm very lucky that it does somehow always seem to work out in the end.

In 2024, I was filming at *EastEnders* and the Christmas tree was up in October. I said to someone, 'This will be the last time I'm here for Christmas.'

They looked at me, worried. 'Don't say that.'

'No, not in a morbid way,' I said. 'It's just that I'm not going to be here next year and I'm not sure if I'm ever going to see it all done up again, which is a shame, because I love Christmas. But I think this is it.'

It felt very final when I left the show. As much as I say that, the door has been left open, which I'm eternally grateful for. People were already saying, at my leaving do, 'When are you coming back? You've got to come back,' and that was lovely, even though anything can happen as we all know. They can kill me off-screen; they can do anything. Maybe the show won't even exist, who knows?

But after all the Christmases I've been there, this felt like a last, fond farewell.

My Christmas cupboard is in my podcast room. It is filled with memories of Christmas that start calling to me as the nights draw in. I love getting out all the boxes of decorations that remind me of years gone by. My mum's angel for the top of the tree; the angel that Eliza made out of a plastic water bottle, I don't know how many years ago now. Eliza's angel is nearly falling apart, but I salvaged it last year, and I love it so much. I love all the decorations that the children have made over the years.

I might add something as the year goes on. I'll slip open the cupboard and pop in a new thing that I've picked up here or there. There's a Christmas shop in Padstow. I like to pop in and have a look when we're down there. Marc says, 'For goodness' sake, you can't be thinking about Christmas in April!' But I might just have to buy a little decoration to tuck away. I can't help myself. Only, the last time I went, it was closed for Easter, and all I could do was peer through the window with sad eyes.

Joanie's got the passion for Christmas, which is lovely to see. It's probably because of me, but she gets super excited when we unpack the Christmas boxes. 'Look at those! I remember that from last year.' She loves seeing all the old decorations come out again.

Eliza has kept her excitement and joy for Christmas too, which I'm so glad about. She loves it. 'The Christmas movies start soon! The Christmas music starts soon!' It's not just Father Christmas, it's everything.

Christmas movies are so important – last year, the girls picked out *Nativity* as the film to watch as we were putting the tree up. It was always going to be *Nativity*, *Elf* or *Home Alone*. Those are the big three in our house.

Our Christmas tree usually goes up the first week of December, but last year I did it a couple of weeks earlier because I knew I was going to be so busy. It was nice to have it up for that little bit longer, lights, baubles and all. To be honest, I think I like the run-up to Christmas even more than the big day itself. It's such a magical time.

I would love to have a real tree, but I can't bear to see it looking sad towards the end of the season, as it inevitably will be, because I have it up for such a long time. And I hate chucking the tree out into the garden. There's something really upsetting about it for me. It's the contrast between seeing the tree at its best, decorated and beautiful, and glimpsing it out in the garden, lying on its side, fading away. I don't like it – I don't like hangovers to things.

I have a Christmas tree in my lounge and another in

my kitchen. The girls each have a Christmas tree in their bedrooms. The tree in my lounge is extremely realistic. It's dressed well, it doesn't drop or make a mess; it just looks pretty. It comes out when I want, and I can put it away when I want, and then use it again next year.

Usually, I do all the trees in one day and it absolutely kills me, but last year I did it differently, and it worked better. I did the lounge tree with a few decorations one weekend, and the girls did theirs the following weekend. It was quite nice spreading it out, not giving myself masses to do. As I've got older, I've learned that you don't need to do everything in one day. It's better to set yourself a task that is enjoyable, rather than give yourself a mountain to climb.

With presents, I try to pick things up throughout the year. If someone says they like something, I'll make a mental note to go back and buy it later. Or if I see something I know they will like, I pop it in the basket. I don't buy for loads of people, but I buy lots of things for the people I do buy for, if that makes sense.

It all depends on the person. With certain family members, I just know their tastes and what they'll like. My brother's sixtieth birthday is coming up and he loves wine, so I've been looking at this brilliant corkscrew system called Coravin. Lots of the big restaurants use it – you can pour one glass of wine from a bottle while the cork stays in, it's amazing. Researching and finding the perfect gift can take a bit of time, but it's something I really enjoy.

I'm not a massive internet shopper unless I know exactly what I'm looking for. For instance, if I know someone likes a certain perfume, and I can get that online, I will. But I prefer experiencing the joy of walking around a shop, especially at Christmas. I love popping into places, wandering around markets or little independent shops, and thinking, 'So-and-so would love that,' when things jump out at me.

I know a lot of people prefer the ease of online shopping and want to avoid the crowds, but if you go at the right times, I think browsing in person is how you find the best things.

I've never been a fan of online shopping to be honest, not even for clothes, although sometimes Maria helps me with that by sending a link to something nice. Honestly though, I find it all a bit much. It hurts my head. I think it's the screen – I just look at it and think, 'Oh God, no, I can't be bothered.'

Don't get me wrong, Amazon is my best friend, like it is for most of us. If something breaks, I grab it there. But I would never browse on Amazon. That would drive me nuts!

Marc is terrible to buy for because he has his interest in the steam engines, and I can never think what else to get him. He's not particularly into his clothes; he wouldn't be wowed if I bought him a designer top for £300. He'd say, 'That's ridiculous. What have you done that for?' In terms of gifts for Marc, I feel like I'm always buying him the same sort of stuff, which annoys me. But then again, if people enjoy what they enjoy, the fact that it's not a novelty is my problem, not theirs. I may be thinking it's boring to buy the same thing again, but if it's something they will actually use and enjoy, then that's great.

Eliza should be easier these days because she's so into

everything – her make-up, perfume and clothes – but it's difficult to buy things without getting her approval first. It's pointless for me to buy her clothes as she will just say she doesn't like them. Teenagers are difficult. It's very rare that I say, 'This is nice,' and she says, 'Yeah, I like that.' More often than not, she'll look at it and go, 'That is disgusting.' So, now, I give her money for Christmas, and then in January we go out and have a lovely day where she can buy what she wants.

By the time June comes along, I'm already thinking that I'd like to start getting organised. In reality though, it never happens. I would love to be able to get to November and have everything bought, but on the first of December I'm always thinking, 'Oh God, I've still got so much to do.'

I love wrapping. Wrapping is brilliant. The gifts from Father Christmas go in lovely, old-fashioned, traditional Christmas paper, which you can usually get from somewhere like HomeSense. They do gorgeous rolls of paper. Joanie's paper is usually decorated with something she's into or something really fun. Eliza gets something a bit more cool. I'll always make sure to wrap their stuff in different papers from each other – I think it's important. Not every single person gets their own paper, but the children in the family definitely do. My nephew always gets something with a dinosaur in a Christmas hat or whatever he is into at the time. The girls will have something fitting for them, and then the older ones usually get all the same.

I love making a whole day out of my wrapping – I'll stick a Christmas film on the telly, pour myself a Baileys, lay everything out, and just have a whole day of wrapping while the kids are at school.

Back in the *EastEnders* days – which already feels like a lifetime ago – it was brilliant because I had a dressing room where I could take all the children's presents so they couldn't find them. I used to come in laden with bags and everyone would say, 'Here she comes, Mrs Christmas is back.' Actually, when I left, a few people said, 'What are we going to do at Christmas without you and your paper and your wrapping? We are really going to miss you being around.'

The shower in the dressing room bathroom, which I never used, would start to pile up with presents. Then, during my breaks, I would do all my wrapping. My wrapping is not bad, but I don't take my time over it. I love the tags, the bows and the ribbons, though. I like all of it, really. There's nothing nicer than looking under a tree at all the gifts and the tags. It just brings me so much happiness.

As well as present wrapping, there's Christmas outfits to think of too. In my wardrobe, there's sequins, black velvet and reindeer jumpers that play music, and I start donning the sparkles from mid-November onwards. The Christmas films will begin rotating around that time, as well; there's a lot of content to get through every year. Then there are the Christmas books to read with Joanie. I've probably got a hundred different Christmas stories, and I'd never get through them all if I started reading them with her in December. Even so, every year I find that Christmas will end and there will still be a few films we haven't watched and Christmassy things we haven't had time to do. I'm not one for going beyond the January deadline, mind you. By the twelfth night, everything needs to be put away and cleaned and done. So, I would rather start it all a little bit earlier and make the most of it all while I can.

On Christmas Eve, I'm at home. Always, always. People laugh because it's an absolute rule with me. 'If you want to pop in and have a glass of champagne, feel free,' I say. 'I'll be cooking.'

I love being at home on Christmas Eve. The carols from King's College, Cambridge are on BBC Two and that's something I like to watch. Even though I've seen *Jamie Oliver's Christmas Eve* preparation a hundred times, I like to watch that every year, as well. Last year, my niece Evie May bought me *Carols from King's* on vinyl. Evie May is very musical. She got a first in music at Clare College, Cambridge, and sang in the choirs while she was there, so we're very proud of her.

It's a family trait, I think, that we can put our minds to things and do them well. We've got common sense and we're confident about putting ourselves forward. I'd say that everyone in the family is naturally expressive, which is good for me, as it wouldn't work to have my family come on the pod if they were shy and didn't want to speak!

The King's College carols sound lovely on vinyl. Last year, we put them on the record player on Christmas morning while we were having our glass of Buck's fizz, Christmas Day being the one day of the year where it's absolutely allowed to get up and have a little alcoholic beverage!

In 1647, and for thirteen long years afterwards, Christmas was banned outright by Oliver Cromwell's government during the English Civil War. Why? Partly because the festivities were thought to encourage drunkenness and debauchery. And their point was . . . ?

The ban was enforced by the New Model Army, who went around making shops stay open on Christmas Day and seizing evidence that people were secretly having parties. How stupid can you be? The quickest way to alienate a population is to stop them from having fun, especially in the middle of winter, when we all need a knees-up to brighten up the mood amidst all that gloom. Some people ignored the rules; others used it as an excuse for a riot; and everyone was thoroughly relieved when in 1660, fun-loving Charles II restored the right to celebrate Christmas again.

A century later, the French had a go at banning Christmas during the French Revolution. From 1917, Russian revolutionaries declared Russia an atheist socialist state and did the same. The suppression of Christmas is still going on in pockets of the world, and the response is always the same. The parties continue secretly, until such a time as they are allowed again. Pointless.

Christmas Day, we all wake up and come downstairs in our pyjamas. Marc and I usually have a cup of coffee with a drop of Baileys in it, or perhaps a nice Buck's fizz. We sit in the lounge, and Marc films the girls coming down the stairs and into the lounge to see what Father Christmas has left. I have four stockings with our names on them, which I hang up in the lounge on stocking hangers, and Father Christmas fills them up down there. Then he can eat his carrots and drink his brandy, and it all happens downstairs. He has lots to do, so I feel it's better for him to stay in one place.

Next, we sit down and go through the stockings. Then I'll probably go into the kitchen and start getting the dinner ready. I might put the potatoes on the boil, have another Buck's fizz, come back into the lounge, then someone will say, 'Why don't you open another present?' It's all lovely and slow and there's no rushing. The girls don't tear everything open at once like I used to as a child, when everything would be done by eight in the morning – all the presents open and finished.

Now, Joanie will open something, and if it's a Lego set or something crafty, she'll say, 'Ooh, I'll open this now,' and I say, 'Do not start the Lego yet. Leave that for a minute. Maybe do it later.'

We always have to have the obligatory bin bag ready so that we can tidy up a bit as we go. The girls might still leave quite a few presents unopened. I do buy a lot, though, it is quite absurd. Marc looks at me as if to say, 'You've done it again.' But bless him, he says well done if he can see I've tried to hold back a bit and he does put up with my odd little Christmas fixation.

The girls will leave some presents for later, play with a few things, and Eliza will go and get ready. Then probably around eleven, I will head up and have a shower, and Marc will have his. Then we might open a couple more bits and bobs.

I am the worst for opening presents. Marc says, 'Open something, open something,' and I say, 'No, no, no.' I will still have presents left at ten o'clock at night that I haven't unwrapped yet. I think it's because I just don't want the day to end.

I know it sounds boring, but I really do mean this – I would be absolutely fine with getting nothing for Christmas. It wouldn't bother me. Watching someone else open a present and seeing their face means so much more to me.

Maybe that's because I've worked all my life, and if I want something, I'll just get it. If you asked anyone in my family, they would probably tell you I'm the worst person to buy for. I have everything already – but I love everything too, so I think I am actually very easy to buy for. You could give me a glass pot, a plant, a candle or a book and I would love it. And I realise that the kids want to see my expression when I open presents, as well, and I am always touched by the thought that other people put into buying too.

We usually get everything going around half past twelve or one o'clock. Everything is on the boil or in the pans and doing well, and then we walk over to the pub for one or two drinks. It only opens for a few hours on Christmas Day, and I love it because everyone is all dressed up. We'll head home after an hour – if my brothers are coming, they might arrive around two or three. Last year we ate around five o'clock. It was a really chilled day and just so enjoyable.

After dinner, we sit at the table. I get the trivia cards out, different quizzes or little bits and pieces, and we play a nice game. We often have a new board game because people know we love them, so we'll play something new, or one we already have, and put on some music. A couple of years ago, I came across a board game called Santa's Rooftop Scramble. 'Well, this is going to be no good because it's Christmas themed,' I thought, but it turns out it's very, very good – brilliant, actually. You help Santa deliver the presents around the board to different families. It's nice that we can't play it all year round; it's a new Christmas tradition and another thing the girls enjoy getting out of the Christmas boxes.

I'd rather not watch a film in the evening because I'll just fall asleep. But last year it was *Gavin and Stacey*, wasn't it? That was huge. We were all waiting for it. It was on quite late and Joanie had gone to bed by then, but the rest of us loved watching it.

Christmas is lovely, especially with the big family we've got. I might have some family over on Christmas Day, then Mark's family might come on Boxing Day, or the other way round. Then maybe on the twenty-seventh or twenty-eighth, I'll see another part of the family and it'll feel like another Christmas Day.

What makes Christmas so wonderful? For me, it's the emphasis on giving that I really like. Everyone is more generous, everyone's in a better mood. It's a sociable time, full of merriment and overindulging, and most of all, it's fun. Getting the family all together, eating a very large roast dinner, pulling crackers, playing board games, charades and watching the King's speech.

Christmas is everything that I am, really; it's everything that brings me joy. I love giving presents to people, I love cooking for people, I love having a drink and a sing-song. I really do just think it's a brilliant time of year!

The Aztecs had five 'lost' days at the end of their calendar year that weren't named after gods, and nobody cared about. I feel like a sense of that has remained with the five days between 27 and 31 December. They feel like some of the only days of the year that have no special meaning and belong to us and us alone. These are days that can be truly restful if you spend them in a cosy fug at home after Christmas is done and dusted. They can be lovely and sociable too, as they are for me, when I'm seeing all the people I want to see and enjoying every minute of the best of all holidays.

Chapter Eleven

Mother's Day

When I was about twelve, I got the bus from Essex Road to Moorgate, where there was a massive M&S. I bought Mum a big bunch of flowers, a vase and some placemats. I really spoiled her, and it felt so nice to do something for her. I've always liked giving presents, and Mum loved it, although I'm sure she probably said, 'You didn't need to do that.' She was a real one for saying, 'Don't be so silly. Don't waste your money.' She didn't need proof of my love for her, but I'm sure it was nice to be shown how much she was appreciated.

I always think of my mum on Mother's Day, so it can be quite a difficult day for me, as it is for anyone who doesn't have their mum anymore. Losing my mother as a teenager was traumatic, and when you experience trauma at such a young age, you often think you're fine. Even when I was thirty, I'd have said to you, 'Oh, my mum dying didn't really damage me.' It's only now that I'm older, and I can look at the shape of my life – the things that have happened and the choices I've made – that I realise that I really was not in a good place.

I made some awful decisions, but bad decisions can come good in the end. I had a lot of heartache in my twenties, and a lot of grief, but maybe everything happens for a reason. I mean, I've got the most beautiful daughter in Eliza. She and Joanie are my world.

It's huge becoming a mum because you're not your first priority anymore. I had Eliza when I was twenty-seven and for me, it was brilliant. I had always wanted to have children, and now I had this amazing little girl in my life to look after, and all the family loved her. Eliza is named after my mum, and Joanie is named after Marc's nan.

There was a period of time when I was on my own with Eliza. I could have really done with having my mum around, of course, but I was very lucky because I had the support of everyone else in my amazing family, especially my nieces and sisters-in-law. There were also plenty of times when it was just me and Eliza in the flat, and we had a lovely time together. I never wanted anything different. I've always felt that you have to play the cards you're dealt and just get on with it. I'm not a 'poor me' person, never have been. Those times when it was just me and Eliza were really special, and we've always kept that bond. It's nice to have such a strong connection between us.

I used to walk with her in the pram, all the way from my flat in Broxbourne up to Brookfield in Cheshunt – a forty-five-minute walk. I'd power-walk up there, give her a bottle in the café, pick up whatever I needed from M&S and walk back. I used to do that three or four times a week if I wasn't working. I absolutely loved those walks. The only thing I'd be thinking about was what time to give her the next bottle.

When Eliza was born, I couldn't stop staring at her, and it was the same when I had Joanie. Every time someone in the family has a baby, it brings it all back. My nephew Dominic had a baby boy this year. He had Amelia first, and now, Frankie Charles – Charles, after my dad. I was holding little Frankie not long after he was born, and as he lay on my chest – this tiny, new little being, so gorgeous – I didn't want to move; I wanted to stay there forever, inhaling the newborn smell of him.

Does that make me sound broody? When people ask if I would like another child, I shake my head. They laugh and say, 'All right, so you're not going to have another one yet . . . but there's plenty of time. You'll change your mind.'

My mum was of course forty-four when she had me, but I don't think another baby is on the cards for me. In my mind, that door has closed, and although I don't want another baby, it's still a scary thing to say that I don't think I'll have another. Sometimes, with all these new babies in the family, I think, 'Oh, I really miss it.' But actually, I'm so lucky because I'm surrounded by babies, which means I can borrow one for the night or have one for a sleepover. I can enjoy cuddling all these beautiful babies and then, when they get to two or three years old and they're running around and you don't get a rest, I can think, 'No, thank you.'

I feel done, and I feel happy with our little family. I also don't think it would be the right thing for me and Marc to do it all over again. We've not had any time on our own as a couple because Eliza was there with me from the beginning.

We had a brilliant time, and I wouldn't change a thing, but I feel like once Eliza and Joanie are grown up, Marc and I are going to have the time that we missed out on back then: the courting, the going out and staying away. We didn't really do any of that, so I'm looking forward to it.

Also, I have reservations about being an older mum, and that's purely down to simple things like the fact that I get really tired. These days, I really do need my sleep. I like the fact that on a Saturday or a Sunday morning, my kids can get up and I don't need to. I like the fact that we can all just get in the car without needing a big bag of stuff. Going out is easy when you don't have to take a pram, nappies, wipes, a change of clothes, snacks and all the rest of it. So, I'm very happy to be a lovely great-auntie, which I am now, to five little ones. I love having them over and I absolutely adore every one of them. They're beautiful, but it's also lovely when they go home. It's nice to shut the door and say, 'Ah, a bit of peace.' Meanwhile, Marc is building a small-scale railway in our garden, and he's panicking. 'I need to get this railway done for the kids!' he keeps saying.

Things were tricky after Eliza was born, but I feel I had Joanie at a really good time because I was settled with Marc and he had a lovely relationship with Eliza, who was nearly six when her sister was born. I was also back at *EastEnders*, where they kindly wrote Sonia out of the script so that I could have maternity leave, knowing I'd be going back when I was ready, after eight or nine months.

Eliza was thrilled to have a little sister. The girls are six years apart, but the age gap between them feels fine – they're not treading on each other's toes, but not too far apart, either. They've always got on really well and adore each other, which I'm so glad about. When Joanie was born, I had my family, of course, and Marc's family, too. Eighteen months later we moved to where we live now, and my dad came to live with us too. The one person missing was Mummy. I really felt the loss of her and still do. I miss having the opportunity to see her, to take her to out and have a coffee or walk around our local garden centre on a sunny day. To be able to phone her up and say, 'I'm off this morning. Shall we go up to M&S and have a walk round?' Or, 'Shall I drive over and have a cup of tea?'

Mum would have been older, obviously, but she would have loved to get to know the children and cook Sunday lunch for us. It's such a shame and I feel I've been robbed of those things.

So, Mother's Day is tinged with sadness for me – although, that said, I do also love it when Joanie and Eliza make me breakfast on a tray while I'm asleep. Joanie gets so excited and her face is a picture of concentration as she carries the tray up to me in bed, careful to keep it steady. Next to my breakfast will be a card she's made at school, along with something she's picked out for me at the garden centre. One year it was a wooden owl, and though it isn't much to look at, it's one of my favourite possessions because she picked it out especially for me.

I've also got some lovely things from Eliza, from when she was younger. Of course, these days she wants to choose something more sophisticated for me. She knows how much I love fancy candles and certain scents, so you've now got poor Marc fielding suggestions for designer perfumes and candles on Mother's Day.

Eliza and Joanie are very strong girls and they both know their own minds. It might make them harder to bring up at times, but I think it's so important for girls to be strong and independent, and I'm so proud of them both. Joanie is nine now; my little girl is becoming a bigger girl and I've really noticed the change. She's become quite defiant and has been shouting at me a lot lately. For me, the key to dealing with any challenge in parenting is to find out why it's happening. Inevitably, I wind up googling things because I find that, once you know the answer and can better understand something, you can accept it and not be so impacted by it.

I did some research, and discovered that Joanie's probably having a surge of hormones, which can start happening around the ages of eight or nine. On the one hand, she's getting older, more grown up and independent, but on the other hand, she still wants her teddy and to be cuddled, so it's a confusing time for her. She needs to grow and learn how to adapt to the changes in her body and brain.

Joanie loves learning. If I ask her what she'd like to play, she'll always chooses 'schools'. She lays out a big mat and gets out her spelling books and games, and then we sit together and do spellings and reading. She won't stop talking for a moment, and I think she really is quite breathtaking.

Eliza has a legal brain. She has this ability to persuade

you that you're sitting on a bean bag even if you know full well that it's a chair. She's very persuasive. She'll make you believe that she hasn't left the straighteners on when you know she has. I'm always telling her that she should be a barrister and go into law, but then again, she'd also make a great TV producer. Honestly, as long as she's happy and earns a living, I'll be proud of her, whatever she does.

I found the early teenage stages fairly difficult with Eliza when she was around thirteen, but now she seems to be on the other side of that, and we get on well at the moment. I'm okay with her growing up; I'm enjoying having a half a glass of wine with her at Christmas. I'm enjoying dropping her and her friend in town wearing their identical low-cut tops and black jeans. I'll enjoy it while I can, because in a few years' time, she'll get her driving licence and be driving herself off and away. These days, I'm constantly looking out for things we can go to together, like the interactive Vogue runway exhibition at King's Cross, which was brilliant. However old your kids are, it's about finding the joy at every stage, because though it's cheesy to say, they really do grow up so fast.

Every now and then the mum-guilt creeps in, though, especially when work commitments mean that I miss important moments along the way.

People say, 'You're so lucky to be on the telly!' And I know I'm lucky financially. I'm not a millionaire, but we do well enough to have nice things. Yet, along with that privilege has come the undeniable fact that no one can ever do my job for me on a sick day, a birthday or a school sports day. I'm not in an office and I can never say, 'Dawn, would you mind picking up that meeting tomorrow and starting that report on the laptop for me, and then I'll carry it on at home?'

No one could ever be me at work when I was on *EastEnders*, and that's the price you pay for working on a long-running TV drama. It was very, very rare that I would ever get to have time off for assemblies or school plays and it was only a stroke of luck when my schedule allowed it.

When the children were younger, I always gave them the same simple explanation: 'Mummy has to work. It's Mummy's job and no one can replace Mummy.'

After a couple of times, they got used to it. Kids are adaptable, and they understand. Nowadays, if I'm there for a school event, it's a huge bonus, but they're fine without me too.

I might feel gutted about it sometimes, but I won't agonise about it in front of them. I will say, 'It'll be brilliant, and I wish I was coming. It's a shame, but that's life.' I'm lucky to have good mum friends at the school who will be there for my kids as well as for their own, taking pictures and praising them if they've been singing or performing. And it goes both ways – I'll do the same for them whenever I can.

I missed so many sports days when I was working at *EastEnders*. Whenever the school announced the date, it would always be too late to apply for a day off and so it didn't happen. But a couple of years ago, for the first year in a very, very long time, it just so happened that I was off, and so was Marc, on Joanie's sports day. We couldn't wait.

At the last minute, I was asked to do a TV interview

down in Cornwall. We were offered a free trip to one of our favourite seaside spots in the world. 'I can't do it,' I said. 'It clashes with our daughter's sports day, and I want to be there.'

It felt like it was going to be a really nice moment for us as a family, and we were all excited.

Then Joanie got chicken pox.

We had to laugh, even though it hurt to miss the one and only sports day we had planned for. But there was nothing funny about not being able to go to Eliza's GCSE options evening a few months later. You shouldn't have to miss something like that – not when you've asked politely for the time off three weeks in advance and got a flat-out no. It felt unfair, because I was never off sick; I rarely missed a day of work in all the years I was on *EastEnders*. And I really needed to be at Eliza's GCSE options evening. I won't miss the next meeting, though . . .

Occasionally Eliza will complain and say, 'You're never here, Mum.'

I know she's being a teenager trying to hurt me. Anyway, it's not true – I'm around a lot. But it makes me feel bad because there are of course times when I'm not around. I can be at home for two weeks solid, but then I can be away for two weeks on the trot, as well.

I have friends who get on the train at seven o'clock in the morning for work and don't get home until after seven in the evening. Yes, they spend time with their kids at the weekend, but there's no variety there. Things are always the same.

Which is better, I wonder? Each week is different for me, and maybe that makes things difficult for my children because there's no routine or consistency for them. Yet maybe my friends' children would prefer that to only seeing their parents at the weekend – who knows? There's such a lot of pressure on women to be able to 'do it all', but realistically, it just isn't always possible. Ultimately, I think there's no right or wrong way of doing these things. We're all doing the best that we can, and so long as kids know that they're loved and supported, and that you are there for them emotionally, I think they'll be okay.

Mums, Kids and Phones

How do we navigate phones and social media? No one seems to have the answer. I had an early insight into the power of YouTube Shorts when Eliza somehow got onto YouTube when she was about three and became obsessed with watching Japanese sweet-making. The sweets expanded when you poured water on them and were modelled to look like sushi or cheeseburgers. Maria actually found them online one year and bought them for Eliza for Christmas – she was ecstatic! What I found odd about the whole thing was the way that she became obsessed with them so quickly at such a young age. After that, I didn't allow her on YouTube, and I've never let Joanie go on YouTube. You learn, don't you, from the first one?

People always comment on my children when they're in a room with adults or older teenagers. 'They're so sociable! They look you in the eye and they can hold a conversation.'

I really believe it's because they don't watch that fast-paced, twenty-second stuff. I may be wrong, but I firmly believe that it's not good for young brains to be immersed in a screen all the time. I'm very wary of what it does to your powers of concentration when you are scrolling through things and seeing things at a very fast pace.

Eliza didn't get a phone until she was in year eight, which was a really tough rule to maintain. I still didn't want her to have it then, but it got too much. At school, they'd do assemblies about phones, and it would be, 'Hands up if you've got a phone,' only for Eliza to be the only one who didn't put her hand up. The assembly was meant to help, but instead it left her feeling very left out.

The first phone she had was an old one of mine – it was cracked, and you could only talk on the phone if you had it on speaker. Then Marc gave her one of his old phones. 'If that goes, I'm not buying you a new one,' I said. 'If there's a spare one around, fine, but until you are working and can afford to have a phone, I am not buying you one. Not doing it.'

Soon, everybody at school was asking for each other's Snap, so before I knew it, Eliza was asking, 'Can I have Snapchat?' That's how they message – WhatsApp is so old-fashioned to them, it's a joke – and so it felt really difficult to withhold it from her. All power to parents who manage to say no, but for Eliza, it would have been too painful for her not to join in. So, eventually I said yes to Snapchat.

I allowed her to get Instagram when she was fourteen. I know a lot of the organisations are looking to ban these platforms for children up until the age of sixteen, but I spoke to Eliza extensively and bored her to tears with it for so long before she got it that I was confident she understood the potential pitfalls.

Her Instagram account is a teen account. It's also on my phone, so I can check it at any time. I'm fully connected; it's as if it's my account. I can see who she's following, the conversations she's having and what she's doing at any time of the day, and I check in on a regular basis.

'How are you finding Instagram?' I said to her, a few months after she got it.

'Hardly go on it,' she said.

She knows how I feel – and I am a dragon about it. 'If I see an inappropriate picture of you, or I see you in conversation with someone I think isn't right,' I say, 'this phone will go. And then you won't have a phone until you can afford your own and you're old enough to sign a contract.'

My advice to other parents would be:

1. Drag it out for as long as you can before they get a phone/get access to social media.
2. Keep boring them to tears about the dangers. I don't think it hurts.

Eliza has TikTok now, and I don't understand TikTok very well, so it's hard for me to check. But you do have to trust them a little bit, I think.

I'd lie to my mum all the time as a teenager, and I don't want Eliza to do that. I'm sure every teenager lies and it's part of growing up, but when it comes to the big things, I really hope that she will confide in me.

I'm very lucky to have my nieces because it means Eliza and Joanie will have other close female relatives they can turn to if they feel the need. There will always be a lot of female support there for them, from Evie May, who has just come out of university, to Ellia and Maria, who are mums now themselves, but of younger kids.

Technologically, I think this generation of parents has been through the most turmoil. During our lifetimes, we've gone from not even having the internet to having dial-up, and now to all this at our fingertips all the time – I think it is a lot. Because of that, I'm really trying to keep the conversation with Eliza open.

I got a message from a *Life with Nat* listener – she was a teacher who wished to remain anonymous. It was World Book Day, and she was getting her eleven-year-old daughter all dressed up for school. 'At the same time,' she said on her voicenote, 'I'm laying out our funeral clothes for the wake this evening of my daughter's friend.'

The friend was also eleven, and she had taken her own life in a situation to do with phones and unkindness on social media. It stayed on my mind, and a couple of days later I played Eliza the voicenote. It wasn't about scaring her; it was about saying, 'This is what happens to people, Eliza. This really is serious, and that is why I go on about phone safety. You have to understand my worry, because these things happen.'

In response, of course, all you get is a roll of the eyes. 'As if I'm going to kill myself. Don't be stupid.' But she does get it, I think.

Phones make life difficult, as well as easy. I'll say to Eliza, 'Get off your phone,' and she'll reply, 'You're on your phone!'

Of course, there are times when I'm on my phone. But Eliza probably thinks I'm doing what she's doing and watching a TikTok of someone licking a lollipop, when I'm actually writing a work email or paying a bill.

There's a mum/friend dilemma that I sometimes ponder: I want Eliza to trust me, I want her to open up to me and talk to me – and I do want to be her friend in some ways – of course, I do. At the same time though, I am the adult, and she is the child, which means that Eliza needs to understand that it's my job to bring her up the best I can and teach her.

Because of that, if I'm honest, I don't really like to hear people saying, 'My daughter is my best friend.'

I've got my own best friends, and hopefully Eliza's got hers. And yes, of course, I'd like for us to be able to have honest, open conversations, but I question whether you can be a best friend to your child and also parent them effectively. Saying that, kids need to feel it's safe to open up, and I can be quite strict and stern at times, so I do also need to relax a bit. I have to remind myself that, although I got on with my dad like a house on fire, we did have our moments over the years, and that I gave my parents a bit of a dog's life when I was Eliza's age. I was terrible: I was rude, and I never wanted to be at home. So, I do have to keep thinking back to that, because I adored them, although I didn't make it very obvious when I was her age!

My brothers didn't move out of home until they could afford to buy, and none of my nieces and nephews have ever rented. They've all stayed at home until very late and then bought places of their own. That's just the way it's gone in our family. Because of that, I don't envisage shoving my kids out when they're eighteen, although they might choose to go off to university or whatever else. My nieces and nephews are still at home in their mid-twenties, and at a time when property is so expensive, that's normal now.

I left home as soon as I could. My mum and dad, as much as I loved them, were very strict because they were that bit older. I loved them, but I always wanted to be out and about once I got to my mid to late teens, which I think is the same for most young people. I was very fortunate that I had a deposit to put down on a little flat, and I was able to get a mortgage. I think my mum would have preferred me to stay at home longer though.

I say it a lot: I carry a lot of guilt when it comes to my mum. I always feel that I wasn't there enough in my teenage years. But I've come to terms with the fact that it was an age thing, and that it's often the case that teenagers don't see much of their mum for a few years.

However, I have forgiven myself for not being there for my mum. When I opened up about it on the podcast, I was amazed by how many messages I had from people saying it had happened to them, and they felt the same. You realise, once you get things out in the open, that nothing you think is the first time it has been thought. It's one of the reasons why I love doing the podcast and why it has been so therapeutic for me.

Judging by the messages people leave, the podcast has been therapeutic for others, as well. I had a lady the other day who said she feels like she's drowning. I looked at her WhatsApp picture and phoned her while I was doing the pod. It happened to be my first-ever solo podcast – I did it entirely alone – and it was another tick off the list. I felt brave doing it on my own.

I phoned her and said, 'For goodness' sake, I can see by your photo that you've got three young boys, and in the picture, they're immaculately dressed with lovely haircuts. And you're telling me you run your own business and work from home. You shouldn't be feeling like you're drowning because you're doing amazingly well.'

Women do have a lot on their plates. On International Women's Day, the poet Donna Ashworth invited me to a lunch with lots of strong, brilliant women, and we were all talking about being a woman in your forties. I'm fortunate that I haven't gone into perimenopause yet. I don't get brain fog or flushes, and my sleep is fine. But the more you talk about it, the more you realise there's a lot to deal with.

Women are navigating hormonal changes from Joanie's age all the way up to the menopause. We go through so much while having to juggle our lives at the same time. We need to talk to each other and share stories and open up about how we're really feeling. Being able to be honest can be really powerful in stopping you feeling like you're going mad or that you're on your own.

When I look back, I remember Mum changing her sheets every day, which must have been because she was having night sweats. After an uncomfortable night, she'd have to jump straight into getting on with the day while also caring for my Nanny Liz. Mum had to deal with my dad's heart attack, her oldest son having a baby, weddings, becoming a grandmother . . . all while navigating the menopause. And yet she never spoke about it. I don't think that silence can be healthy, can it?

I never got to have any really meaningful conversations with my mum about life, possibly because I was too busy getting on with the business of being a teenager, and because I didn't realise how short and precious the time I had with her would be. I make sure I have those conversations with Eliza now though. Even though she might not be interested, I'll still talk to her about it all because I think it's really important.

Mothering Sunday and Mother's Day are two separate ideas that have merged in our minds over the last hundred years or so.

As far back as in medieval times, Mothering Sunday in Britain was traditionally the day you travelled to your old parish and worshipped at your 'mother church' – the church where you had been christened (as everybody was, back then). Mothering Sunday was held on the fourth Sunday of the Christian festival of Lent, and hopefully you'd be seeing your old mum when you went home, although there were no guarantees of any such thing in an era when the average lifespan was a lot shorter.

Mother's Day as we know it originated in 1907 in West Virginia, USA, when Anna Jarvis organised a celebration of mothers at her local Methodist church on the second Sunday in May. Jarvis was carrying on the work of her own mother, a peace activist and suffragist, who had spent many years campaigning for the creation of a 'Mother's Day for Peace', after caring for wounded soldiers during the American Civil War. After the service in Virginia, Mother's Day took off and in 1914, it was made into a national holiday. It was only a matter of time before factory production lines began rattling out 'I heart you, Mom' goodies. But, annoyed by the commercialisation of what had clearly been a sacred idea for her, Anna Jarvis then campaigned to have Mother's Day taken off the calendar!

From Japan to Mexico, Mother's Day is a big deal around the world. But nowhere tops Ethiopia for its celebration of motherhood, where mothers and Mother Earth are celebrated during a hugely important three-day festival at the end of the rainy season.

One very memorable Mother's Day for me was 31 March 2019. It was wet and cold – the sort of day where all you really want to do is stay in and cook a Sunday roast for your partner and kids – and against my better judgment, I was setting off to do an eighteen-mile run in the pouring rain. The London Marathon was only four weeks away and I needed to get my training in.

Now, I'm not a runner. I'm really, really not a runner! If I say yes to something, though, I'm going to see it through and give it 110 per cent. As I'd said yes to running the London Marathon on 28 April, and this was my only free day for a while, I needed to go out and train in the rain, Mother's Day or not.

It was all Scott Mitchell's fault – Scott, my friend, and now agent, who was Barbara Windsor's husband. Barbara, God rest her soul, was still with us in 2019, but she was battling with Alzheimer's, and she and Scott had become the faces of the Dementia Revolution, a joint campaign between Alzheimer's Research UK and the Alzheimer's Society.

The first I heard of it was when Scott told me that Dementia Revolution had been selected to be Charity of the Year for the London Marathon. He was getting a group together to run and raise money for the campaign. Officially, they were 'Barbara's Revolutionaries', but he was calling them 'Babs' Army' and he asked me to join. How could I possibly say no?

A large group of us signed up from *EastEnders*: among us were Adam Woodyatt, Jake Wood, Emma Barton, Jamie Borthwick, Tanya Franks, Kellie Shirley and Jane Slaughter. Babs' Army went on to raise £150,000 to fund pioneering research at the UK Dementia Institute. The Dementia Revolution campaign went on for an entire year, and raised an incredible £4 million.

I honestly think the hardest bit of the marathon is the

training. It has to be done, though, whether you're in the mood for it or not. It's a bit like work – you set yourself a task and you go and do it. My marathon journey started in January 2019, when I went to a trainer shop, had my feet and gait checked, and bought proper running shoes that supported me and gave my feet stability over a long distance. I didn't undergo any formal training, but I learned a lot from reading books and listening to podcasts about running.

Before 2019, I was someone who would say, 'I can't run,' but I've realised that absolutely anyone can run, if they want to. Of course, you need to start slowly. You run up to the lamp post, then you walk before running up to the next lamp post. The next time you go out, you can run the distance of both of those lamp posts. Before you know it, you're chatting to someone and saying, 'Well, the first hour is tough, but once you get into it, it's quite meditative . . .' and you're thinking, 'Is this really *me* talking?'

Babs' Army had a group WhatsApp where we swapped information and logged our training runs. We messaged each other about Epsom salt baths, protein shakes, electrolytes and staying hydrated. People would pop up with a new tip or nugget of info every day; we were a collective pushing each other on, and it was brilliant to feel like part of a team.

I trained a lot on my own down by the river near our house and after a while, I found that I was really into it. You get obsessed when you're doing a marathon; it's all you can think about. 'When am I running? What should I be eating? When should I be resting?'

And that's how I came to find myself, soaked to the skin, pounding along down by the water's edge on Mother's Day 2019. I ran for eighteen miles, and when I got home, Marc had made a roast. What a treat. It was delicious – although not as good as mine, obviously!

My dad was very supportive throughout my training. He was still well then, and if Marc wasn't in, he'd make my protein shakes for me and when I got back after a run, he'd say, 'I've run you a bath, Squirt.' He wasn't all that good with words, my dad, but it was through his actions that he showed how he felt about you.

The day of the London Marathon arrived, and I knew I would have to be brave. 26.2 miles is a long old way to run, but it helped to visualise the finish line and repeat to myself, 'You can do it.'

I thought about Barbara and Scott as I ran, about all the people with dementia, their friends and family. I thought about my family and friends, who were in the crowd cheering me on, and I wanted to make them proud. I ran slowly, and it took me five hours and twenty-seven minutes to go the distance. It was truly an amazing feeling when I crossed the finish line – I was on cloud nine. I had pushed myself to achieve something I never thought in a million years I could do.

I hurt afterwards, though. I couldn't walk up and down stairs very well; I was like a mechanical wooden toy that hasn't been oiled. But the following day was a Monday morning, which meant, sore legs or not, I was due at work at *EastEnders*, so I just had to get on with it. No time off, remember!

On the whole, I really did enjoy the experience of running the marathon, and you can't help but feel pleased with yourself that you've actually done it – not to mention all the money raised for such an important cause. The training is so arduous and time-consuming though, and afterwards I thought, 'Never again.'

So, when a few of Babs' Army got together again, four years later, and Scott asked me to join them and run another London Marathon, you'd have thought I would have turned him down flat. I'd done it once – I had nothing to prove. Why would I go through all of that again? And yet something in me went, 'Oh . . . just do it . . . go on.'

So, in 2023 I ran my second London Marathon for Alzheimer's UK. This time I did it in five hours, twenty-eight minutes – one minute slower than in 2019! What are the chances of that?

Again, the training was a huge commitment, and after that second marathon in 2023, I gave up running altogether. I can't even run 5K at the moment. What my marathons proved to me, though, was that if I put my mind to something, I will do it, and that's the point.

In 2025, my nephew Dominic was running the London Marathon for the first time. Dom is much more competitive than I am, and even though he'd only ever run 5K before he signed up, he trained really hard, and was aiming to do it in under four hours. I was tracking him all morning on the app, watching the coverage on the BBC, and getting all emotional imagining him on the starting line. There's such an amazing buzz you get being surrounded by all those people doing something truly amazing.

The 2025 London Marathon was one of the hottest on record, but because it was Dom's first time, he had no idea. I could tell from the app that he was flying round, and it looked like he was on track to smash his goal of finishing in under four hours. We were all planning a get together to celebrate his achievement that night, and the whole family was so proud of him. Little did we know what was about to happen.

Just before the end of the race, the wheels came off for Dom. His eyes went funny, then his legs went, but he kept pushing through. He ended up collapsing on another runner – a really kind woman who helped him cross the finish line. The next thing he knew, he was waking up in a bag filled with ice with no idea where he was, what his name was, anything. Terrifying. Bless him, the first thing he asked was whether he'd finished the race, but he had his medal on, so he'd done it!

I think we're all used to seeing people running marathons and things on social media these days, so it's easy to forget what a huge undertaking it is and how much strain you're putting your body under – and that's not even taking into account the heat.

Thankfully, Dom was okay in the end, and the medics at the marathon were amazing and took brilliant care of him. He had to go to hospital and was on a drip until about 3 a.m., but he did it. I popped down with a McDonald's at about 9 p.m., but it wasn't quite the celebration we'd had in mind! I'm so proud of him, and he did manage to do it in under four hours, in spite of everything. I know how much of a commitment the training is, and Dom has two young kids and a full-on job. He also absolutely smashed his fundraising target, and raised so much money for the homeless charity, Shelter, which is incredible.

Apparently, only 0.01% of the population have completed a marathon, but it is something I'd recommend to anyone, no matter how fast or slow you do it in. If you've got a charity that's close to your heart, go for it! It is such a mental challenge as much as a physical one, though your toenails do take a bit of a bashing.

If Scott asked me again, it wouldn't be a definite no, but these days, as much as it takes double the time to burn the calories, I prefer walking. I think it's better for your bones. Walking, Pilates and a little bit of strength training is really what you need as a woman coming into the perimenopause. Best of all is a walk along a country lane with a good friend, which doubles as a counselling session and a workout all in one.

Mother's Day is also a chance for me to shout out to all the brilliant mums in my life. Firstly, to my niece Maria, who is a brilliant mum to Alfie and Ruby. Maria works so hard; she has a full-time job and juggles everything so well. Shout out to Maria, in every way. She is amazing.

To Ellia, my niece, who is a new mum. She's got baby James, and she is just the best mum. It's so beautiful to watch, because Ellia was always a bit of a free spirit, travelling around with her partner Jack – they were quite an independent couple, doing what they wanted – and now their beautiful baby has come along and they're just amazing parents and it's clear they absolutely love it. So, Ellia is another super mum.

Lastly, to my friend Abigail, who is a really wonderful mother. Not only has she got four children, one of whom has been really poorly, but she has also started her own business on the side doing facials. All her kids are so smartly turned out every day as well – it's just ridiculous and I have no idea how she does it. Abigail is a true super mum.

I also have to mention Linda, Sharon, Sophie, Julia and Rach – you're all just brilliant. Women rock!

Lastly, to all the mums out there who put things aside for special occasions – don't! I think that whatever you buy you should use, and when you're given a gift, you should enjoy it. Take an expensive scented candle, for instance. Don't put it away in a cupboard and save it. A candle loses its scent, so burn it now. Open that bottle of champagne. Relish it. What are you waiting for? Use that really special make-up – otherwise it will go off. The mascara will dry out. The perfume will go bad. Open it now; it will bring you pleasure – and you deserve it. Life is for living, people. Don't forget it.

Tomorrow

Time goes so fast, doesn't it? The days speed by and I honestly don't know where this year's gone. It's crazy. We race through life; we're on a treadmill, rushing around, ticking stuff off and getting things done or worrying about what needs to be done. Then, all of a sudden, a year ago feels like it was yesterday, and tomorrow comes before you've even registered that it's today.

That's when we need to stop, take a moment, and remember why we're here. To take it all in before we find ourselves in a care home. We're only on this incredible planet for a short time, people! It's important to make the most of it, because what's the point of doing it all if you're not actually enjoying it?

The first thing I did every morning when I was in Cornwall earlier in the year was go to the big picture window in our holiday apartment and look out over the sea. Some mornings, the sun was shining, the water glittering and dancing; other days there were storm clouds on the horizon, or it was so dull and overcast that you couldn't see the line between sky and sea. But it was always beautiful – and honestly, I think that is true of life.

I could have been quite a bitter, miserable forty-year-old: I've lost both my parents; I've had a traumatic relationship. I've been through a fair bit in the press with journalists giving me ticks and crosses and being mean. I think that no matter what life throws at you though, it's good to take it on the chin and still have a laugh. My approach to a difficult situation is try to think of the good things – even if it's just the basics that we take for granted, like a roof over our heads, food, warmth and hot water. All the things that we're very, very lucky to have each day.

This year has been brilliant for me. I made the choice to leave *EastEnders* and it honestly couldn't have gone any better. When it was first reported that I was leaving, people asked, 'What's she going to do next?' and I got the odd comment from an acquaintance or two at work who said, 'I'll be seeing you soon,' before I'd even left the show. But this year has shown me that you don't have to be typecast, even if you've done the same thing for ages, and it really isn't the case that nothing else will happen for you.

In fact, so much has happened and so many positive things have been going on that it has made me even more certain that we all need to try new stuff and take chances in life – it's scary, but you have to listen to your heart and your gut – and jump in with both feet!

When you're too busy, it can all become a bit overwhelming, though. I've realised that I need to give myself time to pause, let things sink in and be grateful for them – I think everybody does. Give yourself permission to stop and indulge a little.

Imposter syndrome pushes you to stretch yourself – that niggling little voice that says, 'Take all your chances now, because it won't last for long!' But life is as much about the choices you make as the things you do. I've been lucky enough to do some amazing things, but I've tried to be sensible and not say yes to everything because if I did, I'd never be at home or see my family, and I don't want to dilute myself, either.

I'm a firm believer in being kind to others, but it's also vital that you take the time to be kind to yourself. Otherwise, your brain gets full and your body starts to run down – and then you're no good to anyone. This year is probably the first year that I've really been a bit more aware about looking after myself. I'm not saying I'm doing very well at it, but at least I'm thinking about it now – cutting down on the booze, eating better, trying to move my body and get some exercise in. Saying that, I haven't moved for ages because I've been so busy, but I'm still aware of it! We want to try and live for as long as we can, don't we? Chance plays a part, and maybe our days are numbered from the day we're born, and it's all written in the stars. But if that's not the case, we can help ourselves along a little bit. It's something to try and think about, anyway: look after yourself and take care of your body, so the soul can continue in it.

When life gets manic and the days feel like they're flying past too quickly, remember that there are different ways you can think about time. Yes, the way we measure it is linear – one second follows another, cause comes before effect, yesterday is behind us and tomorrow is ahead. But in science, time is affected by speed and gravity (consult Einstein about this . . .) so it's relative; in our minds, it is layered, looped and elastic, because we're living in the past and the future while we navigate the present; and in stories, it does tricks like a circus performer through your imagination.

There are loads of states of mind that can bend our perception of time: anticipation, boredom, love, tiredness and memory are just some of them – not to mention a gin and tonic! Having a couple of days off every now and then to process things can go such a long way in making life seem longer and richer. Honestly, sometimes you just need to spend a day in bed, or have an afternoon snooze, or go to bed early one night. Sleep is so important. Lie-ins too – even if you're in that lovely, dozing, half-awake state.

It's lovely to know that the door is still open for me at *EastEnders*. Sonia's gone off in a really nice way, and that feels good. But I'm also really enjoying just being me, just being Nat, for now. Amidst everything that's going on, I would like to end this book with a shout out to my lovely readers – that's you! – as well as to the *Life with Nat* pod community and to all the people that follow me on Instagram and can be bothered to listen to my mumbo jumbo. I thank all of you wholeheartedly for following the road I'm on and supporting me all the way and enjoying it so much. I hope there's loads more to come!

Acknowledgements

It really does take a village, and there are so many brilliant, wonderful people to thank!

Marc – thank you for putting up with me, and for your constant support, love and laughter. I couldn't do it without you.

Thank you to my editor, Marleigh. From that very first Zoom call up until now, it's been so much fun.

To my brilliant agent and dear friend, Scott, thank you for making everything happen, and always being on that email, even if it is after 7 p.m.!

To the wonderful Rebecca, thank you so much for everything. I really couldn't have written this book without you.

Huge shout out to all the team at HQ – thanks for making this book a reality!

To Anna Scher, thank you for being the best teacher in the world.

Thank you to Tony and Julia for creating *EastEnders*. What would I have done without you?

A special mention here to my Soph. Sometimes you find

someone who just gets you. You might be halfway round the world, but you'll always be the one I share it all with.

To my darling family:

Maria and Els, I don't really need to say much. Without you both, life is as dull as dishwater. Thank you for the laughter, the constant banter and the love. I am so proud of you both.

Dom – you're a cracker and my handsome nephew, always. I am so very proud of everything you're doing.

James – I always appreciate our conversations, laughs and drinking expeditions. So proud of you.

Evie – you continuously astound me with your work ethic and attitude. You are truly amazing and I'm so proud.

And then to the mothers and fathers of the ones above!

I couldn't be luckier to have two brothers like you pair – and then you went and married your beautiful wives!

David, to quote, as we looked at each other during your sixtieth celebrations in your kitchen in July, we really are very, very lucky. Love you.

Tone, thank you for always being proud of me – and always saying it from the heart. You've been a constant support and we do have a laugh. Love you.

Linny – you've been there throughout it all and I thank you for always being at the end of the phone – even if it is for two hours. Laughter and tears – you're my sister.

Sharon – fashion queen and fab mum, I've learned so much from you over the years. Thank you.

Mummy and Daddy, thank you for making me! I hope I've made you both proud.

To all the amazing women in my life – you know who you are. Thank you for always being there for me, even in those times when I'm too busy to see you. Love you all.

To all of my lovely listeners to the pod and followers on Instagram – thank you. Without you all, I wouldn't be here now.

And lastly, to my beautiful, strong, funny, clever girls, Eliza and Joanie. I love you more than you'll ever know, and I'm so proud of you both.